A LOND

A London Address

The Artangel Essays

GRANTA

Granta Publications, 12 Addison Avenue, London W11 4QR

First published in Great Britain by Granta Books 2013

A CIP catalogue record for this book is available from the British Library.

1 3 5 7 9 10 8 6 4 2

ISBN 978 1 84708 833 8

Typeset in Bembo by Lindsay Nash

Printed and bound in Great Britain by T J International, Padstow

Contents

Introduction

I caught myself listening on tiptoe for the next beat of
the boat ...

Joseph Conrad, *Heart of Darkness*

With London's Olympic year visible on the edge of the horizon,
Living Architecture and Artangel embarked on a collaboration
that would conjure up a boat beached on the top of a building
high above the Thames.

We imagined a space which would work both as a one-
bedroom hotel for private booking by members of the
public and as a studio and observatory for artists, musicians
and writers. An international architectural competition for A
Room for London was launched with an open brief for the site
on the roof of the Queen Elizabeth Hall at London's Southbank Centre, offering panoramic views taking in the City of
London and St Paul's to the east and Big Ben and the London
Eye to the west; at the epicentre of the city, yet gently removed
from its urgent bustle.

David Kohn Architects, in collaboration with artist Fiona
Banner, won out with their *Roi des Belges,* a boat-shaped
installation that took its name from the paddle steamer Joseph
Conrad captained up the Congo River, setting sail from the
Thames at Gravesend in 1890. We know from Conrad's diary
and *Up-River Book* that it was his experience of this attritional

journey that inspired the story and setting for *Heart of Darkness,* published just at the end of the century.

Craned in place overnight in mid-December 2011, before opening to guests at the start of the New Year, Kohn and Banner's *Roi des Belges* teetered over the edge of the building as if washed up by the high waters of a receding flood.

The Artangel programme established a monthly rhythm that navigated us through the Olympic Year of 2012, both on board and online. Guests to the beached vessel included musicians such as Amadou and Mariam, Jarvis Cocker, Baaba Maal, Imogen Heap and Natalie Clein, each contributing to *Sounds from a Room* – a series of live streamed performances above the river, relayed on to large screens in the Southbank Centre below and small screens around the world. Londoners with an original idea for how to improve their city were encouraged to come forward, and each month the selected idealist was invited to develop their *Idea for London* over a working dinner on the boat, followed by the chance to sleep on it. Other stowaways included Luc Tuymans, whose painting *Allo!* was inspired by Gauguin, another figure who had stationed himself in a far-flung outpost of empire at the end of the nineteenth century, in Tahiti; Roni Horn, who created a litany on water in general and the River Thames in particular; and Brian Cox, whom Fiona Banner directed in the very first performance of Orson Welles's unmade screenplay of *Heart of Darkness* in its entirety, live-to-camera.

Above all, the Conrad legacy gave a clear pointer to the thirteen writers invited to undertake *A London Address.* Marooned on their own in a boat on a roof, silently set apart from the flow of life teeming outside the windows and portholes and the inexorable forward-motion of the tireless Thames below, each writer started with a blank sheet and a special vantage point. In *Heart of Darkness,* Marlow recounts his tale of a journey deep into the darkness of empire from the setting of a boat moored at Gravesend on the Thames. The thirteen writers each completed their pieces in this strange cabin overlooking the same river, and shared them with the world through a podcast recorded prior to disembarking.

The brief to each writer was as fluid as the water below: think about London in 2012 and its place in the world more than a century after Conrad's terrifying dissection of the mindset of empire. Few pieces actually refer directly to the Olympic Games or to the Diamond Jubilee pageant that processed down the Thames and past the *Roi des Belges* in June; instead they look beyond immediate reality to places within and afar, from differing cultural perspectives, recounted through a merging of memory, history and imagination. Differing views from the inside out and the outside in, each piece of writing connected to the others by its unusual physical location, float-ing yet rooted.

Each writer travelled up and down the side of the building in the same slow-moving lift, stepped out over the walkway past the weather station, the wind turbines rotating on the masthead, and ascended the loft-ladder to the small octagonal library. On the desk, two pairs of binoculars; on the wall, a map of the Thames and a map of the Congo. Twin tide timetables in Day-Glo orange; a cabinet containing a portrait of King Leopold, *roi des Belges*, and behind it, a mirror. On the table, the ship's log, big as a bible, inviting each guest to record daily conditions, both internal and external. And next to it a wooden jigsaw puzzle of the *A–Z Street Atlas* – each piece a different London address.

James Lingwood / Michael Morris
Co-directors, Artangel

Juan Gabriel Vásquez

Remember the Future

I have come to the river, to this steamboat run ashore on the
rooftops of London, 121 years and 172 days after Captain Józef
Teodor Konrad Korzeniowski, on board SS *Roi des Belges*,
wrote these instructions:

> Low land and outlying sandbanks a little to port.
> Steering for a little square white patch. Stick on it.
> Pass close to the sands – *Cautiously!*

But that was another river. We think of it, the old Congo River,
as going into the heart of Africa, whereas the Thames goes
out, out from London and into the world. There's a distance
between the two rivers, and it is not geographical. One has to
be cautious when measuring it.

Cautiously I measure the distance I have covered to get here.
It is the distance between Bogotá, the city of my birth, perched
8,000 feet above sea level in the middle of the Andes, and the
city I see through these fourteen windows, in which (according
to Conrad) men and sea interpenetrate. It is also the distance
between my country, former subject of an empire on which the
sun allegedly never set, and this country I write from, former
head of an empire about which Conrad once made the same

7

claims. Finally: it is the distance between my first reading of *Heart of Darkness*, when I had just turned sixteen, and the most recent one – the ninth or tenth: I have lost count – which I began a couple of hours ago, having just been shown to my quarters for the first time aboard my steamboat. My steamboat on the roof, from whose stern I dominate large stretches of this river and this city that are, in their very own way, inscrutable fictions.

Our favourite novels are like buildings we know well: who lives where, where do which stairs lead, how do you reach the basement. Today, however, *Heart of Darkness* is not a building, but a steamboat in which I've been sailing all my writing life and whose private geography – its pilot house, its cabin, its mess room – I know as well as the house I grew up in. In 1899, in three magazine instalments between February and April, Conrad published this story that I now read as the calling card of a prophet of the twentieth century. To my mind, its publication inaugurated a supernatural decade in which Captain Korzeniowski presciently explored every tension and tribulation of the years to come. In *Through the Looking Glass*, Lewis Carroll makes the White Queen say this: 'It's a poor sort of memory that only works backwards.' I remember these words and can't help thinking Conrad was one of those rare novelists who are able to remember the future. Here, about to sail without sailing, I lay out the evidence of his vision on my octagonal desk: three novels as three crystal balls.

It is night now. The shape of the desk, architect David Kohn told me, is taken directly from a scene in Conrad's *Lord Jim*. I find it; Jim and Marlow sit around an octagonal table talking about hell. Conrad writes: 'The night, glittering and sombre, seemed to hang like a splendid drapery'. My London drapery is fully lit: the National Theatre is red; the London Eye is white and blue. Conrad writes: 'The riding lights of ships wink afar like setting stars.' And there are ships on the Thames, but they are quiet and dark and still. I climb to my steamboat's deck to look at the sky, but all I see is a cloud covering the illuminated city, a cloud whose darkness, as the darkness of the blind, is never perfect.

DAY 2: *Heart of Darkness*
TIDE AT 01.30: 6.7 m

Jetlagged, I wake up a little before two in the morning and read Marlow's story under the creamy light of the small bulbs set over my bed. After three hours of hallucinatory reading, my eyes hurt and words have begun jumping off the page. I blame it on my imperfect vigil, my impaired attention, my excited sensibility. Marlow has just talked about his 'battered, twisted, ruined tin-pot steamboat'. I get out of bed; I turn on every light in my own steamboat — it is not so twisted, it is hardly battered — and I start walking around with the novel in one hand and a photograph of the original *Roi des Belges* in the other. I lie down on the wooden floor: this is the part of the deck where Marlow 'seemed to see Kurtz for the first time'. I walk up the metallic stairs to the pilot house where Kurtz's life began, in Conrad's words, 'ebbing out of his heart into the sea of inexorable time'. But I'm unable to make up my mind about the cabin. Where would it be? The cabin, of course, is where Kurtz would pass judgement on his own past and, at the same time, on our impending future: 'The horror! The horror!'

In Conrad's manuscript there was only one exclamation: dread was singular. The doubling of the words in the final version is what has branded them in our reader's memory, what has earned for them a permanent space in our mythology.

After hearing those words, after watching the hideous transformation of the dying man's ivory face in the half-light, Marlow blows out the candle and leaves the cabin. In the mess room he meets the rest of the crew. They are dining and he joins them. It is then that a young boy appears in the doorway and announces, with words T. S. Eliot would later steal: 'Mistah Kurtz – he dead.' Everyone else runs to see the body; Marlow stays, pretending to eat, but it is fear that holds him back, an atavistic fear. 'There was a lamp in there – light – don't you know – and outside was so beastly, beastly dark.' I have never read those lines without a slight shudder, an intimate, shared terror. Now, in my steamboat on the roof, I turn off the lights, all the lights; in the depth of night, exhaustion fills my consciousness with an unreal silence. And suddenly there they are, the images of Conradian horror as interpreted (or understood) by an American film: the Vietnam war, the burned bodies of children, Wagner's music as background for bombings, and that ox clubbed to death with a machete, its grey back broken, the black blood staining the yellow ground. In *'Exterminate all the Brutes'*, Sven Lindqvist highlights the secret liaison between the European colonization of Africa and the Holocaust. Conrad's little book is a yardstick against which we can measure our experience, the experience of a century.

DAY 3: *Nostromo*
TIDE AT 14.42: 7 m

It is raining heavily on the river outside; inside, Conrad talks to me about my country and my continent, their convulsive history. Our relationship changed with my reading of *Nostromo*, Conrad's 1904 novel about the fictitious Latin American republic of Costaguana. Like all great novels, *Nostromo* allows for multiple interpretations, but for me it is and always will be a roman-à-clef about the national traumas of Colombia. I read it for the first time during a long Belgian winter, wondering how was it possible that a Pole writing from England could make me feel the humid heat of the Caribbean coast. In the novel, the province of Sulaco secedes from the republic of Costaguana with the military aid – or is it the intervention? – of the United States; in history, the province of Panama secedes from the republic of Colombia with the military aid – no: the intervention – of the United States.

The real-life events took place in November 1903, while Conrad was writing the novel. American interests in the Panama Canal played a crucial role in the revolution; where history was yelling *Panama Canal*, Conrad whispered *silver mine*, and the barter, the wonderful barter of fiction, was accomplished. Some time before Christmas, Conrad wrote to his friend Robert Cunninghame Graham: 'And apropos, what do you think of the Yankee Conquistadores in Panama? Pretty, isn't it?'

Our long and sad century saw the place name in that (falsely) casual sentence substituted many times: Nicaragua, Honduras, Haiti, the Dominican Republic, Cuba, Guatemala and Chile suffered, albeit in different ways, the consequences of the Monroe doctrine. I turn to the novel and find the ominous words of a millionaire by the name of Holroyd:

> Time itself has got to wait on the greatest country in the whole of God's universe. We shall be giving the word for everything: industry, trade, law, journalism, art, politics, and religion, from Cape Horn clear over to Smith's Sound, and beyond, too, if anything worth taking hold of turns up at the North Pole. And then we shall have the leisure to take in hand the outlying islands and continents of the Earth. We shall run the world's business whether the world likes it or not. The world can't help it – and neither can we.

Reading *Nostromo*, I run into don José Avellanos, the man who is arguably the moral conscience of Costaguana. In the novel he receives the treatment reality (Latin American reality, at least) usually affords to moral consciences: general contempt and a premature death. Don José is modelled after a very real Colombian living in London in 1903: Santiago Pérez Triana, ambassador plenipotentiary, son of an exiled ex-president and the author of books for children. And I can't help thinking that in these moments, on board my steamboat watching the Thames turn white under the pale light, I am a Colombian interpreting London through Conrad, just as in 1903 Pérez Triana, a foreigner in London, helped Joseph Conrad interpret Colombia.

DAY 4: *The Secret Agent*
TIDE AT 09.53: 0.5 m

This will be my last day on board. I climb up to the pilot house
and go out to the deck. The river today is brown, the colour
of these leafless trees; the morning light is scant and the smell
of rain is in the air. When did Joseph Conrad see this view for
the first time? What did he see when he saw it? I read *The
Secret Agent* and cannot help but feel Conrad was a stranger to
London, in much the same way that I am a stranger; perhaps
this is why I have always felt a certain affection for the London
of *The Secret Agent*, for its ghostly, artificial qualities, for its
tourist-guide insights. But great novels are more intelligent
than their authors: they see more, they see better; at their best,
the books we call classics are Pandora's boxes whose warnings
tend to be vindicated by history. One of the most fearsome
characters in *The Secret Agent* is Mr Vladimir, theoretician of
terrorism, who at some point suggests a series of ideal outrages:
'Let them be directed against buildings, for instance,' he says.
On two conditions: first, the said buildings must be a 'fetish'
recognized by 'all the bourgeoisie'; and second, the terrorist
attack must be an act of a 'destructive ferocity so absurd as to
be incomprehensible, inexplicable, almost unthinkable; in fact,
mad.'

I was not in London when the twin towers of the World
Trade Center fell in September 2001; but later, when the
beginning of the war in Iraq was broadcast live on television,
I watched it from a friend's living room near the Emirates
Stadium. Like many, I thought the war was a mistake; like
many, I regretted the atrocities of Abu Ghraib; like many, I was

wounded by the images of the red bus torn apart on 7 July; like very few, I remembered the all too believable words another terrorist pronounces in the novel:

> To break up the superstition and worship of legality should be our aim. Nothing would please me more than to see inspector Heat and his likes take to shooting us down in broad daylight with the approval of the public. Half our battle would be won then; the disintegration of the old morality would have set in in its very temple.

To what extent did they achieve this, those who attacked New York and London?

I do not yet have the answer. But I will not stop asking the question.

Once again I ascend the metallic stairs to the pilot house, but this time I close the trap door behind me and climb the ladder through the hatchway and go out, out to the upper deck, where the wind blows harder and the rain hurts my face, and I remember, looking at the city, that the 7 July bombings took place the day after London was chosen to host the 2012 Olympics. And I say to myself: now the year has arrived. And I say to myself: it is good to be here.

Jeanette Winterson

A Place Before the Flood

Was there ever such a place? The Bible story is simple; God destroyed the wicked world and only Noah and his family were saved. After forty days and forty nights the ark came to rest on Mount Ararat, and as the flood waters began to subside, it stayed there.

Imagine it – evidence of an impossible moment, marooned like a memory point above time. The thing couldn't have happened, but it did – look, here's the boat, part miracle part madness.

I have been using myself as a slow shutter speed camera. Tuesday night 8 p.m. till midnight. Wednesday night midnight till 3 a.m. Thursday night I set the alarm to wake at 3 a.m. and keep watch until sunrise.

What am I watching? Whatever there is.

The day is the day – the tide of people flowing over the tide of the river. The inland rush of busyness. The day it rained the people dried up. The next day the rain dried up and the people flooded the bank again. They don't often look up. This boat balances above them, watching, whether I am here or not. The boat is a witness of everything that happens and the boat itself bears witness to the unspeakable strangeness of life.

Strange, because life is an unseaworthy boat, easily grounded, quick to capsize. Unspeakable because – there's a copy of Beckett in the boat: *Happy Days* – 'There is so little that one can say that one says it all'.

Unspeakable life. And it does seem so, perched here in a boat perched here on a roof and myself at slow speed, non-digital.

A thousand thousand frames and what shall I write on the bottom of each one?

On the walls of the Hayward Gallery behind me there's a drop-down sign: LIFE IS TO BLAME FOR EVERYTHING.

1.45 a.m. Thursday morning. Two kids on bikes down below doing mime. She's miming a fish. The other kid is irritating her so she swallows him like he's Jonah and she's the Whale. The size of a whale's arteries are so big that a child could crawl through them. A whale is not a fish – a whale is a mammal. Do you remember the one that swam into the Thames? Here he comes, bucking the boats out of the water. Breaking the bridge in half.

On Waterloo Bridge there are as always – and I know that now – people walking home whatever the hour. Waterloo Bridge flows across the river – its own cross-current of north to south. There is never a pause. The prevailing wind is westerly. Yesterday half my boat was drenched, the other half dry. Tonight – or this morning, whatever it is – there is the sight of nearly a dozen rickshaws slowly pedalling south across the river; finished with tourists and drunken lovers, the boys are all going home. The wind suddenly beats across the bridge at its most exposed. The rickshaw boys curse and crouch lower.

It is 2.15 a.m. The police boat passes.

The day I came on this boat I had been writing about *Titanic*. Joseph Conrad hated *Titanic* – he said she looked like a Huntley and Palmer's biscuit tin. He had a manuscript of his on board when *Titanic* went down – he was sending it to sell to a New York dealer.

The sea wasn't safe, thought Conrad, and that was one good reason to be on it. At sea, whatever you are, whatever you really are, will soon begin to show.

It is odd that we spend so much of our lives in disguise from one another.

Last night, soon after midnight, there was a couple rowing. As I write it I see that rowing and rowing look the same and as they were on the river and so am I, perhaps it was both. They were rowing away from each other, that's for sure. He walked off, leaving her at the rail looking into the full water. She turned, leaning, lighting a cigarette, angry, stiff. The vagrant I've seen a lot, with the Jack Russell terrier, wandered by, unmoved by wind or tears. He was talking to himself or the dog. 'Goodnight, Lady,' he shouted.

Tonight it's much quieter because it is so late or so early. I never know what to say about the small hours – except that they are small. Time curls up. Time slows down. Only an idiot thinks that one moment is the same length as another. Across from the boat there are a few lights still on in the bedrooms of the Savoy Hotel.

I suppose they can see me, lit up, speculative, kneeling up to see out of the window, looking for clues. God, the river is high and dark – an old river, centuries pumped into it. The Romans sailed up this river when the banks on either side were densely wooded and wild beasts came down at dusk to drink. There were mammoths on the river once – giants that time played a trick on, smuggling them out of life and into imagination. There he is, lumbering under the arch of the bridge, pushing through time like water. The past always present. Liquid history.

Time the river. 'What will you do now with the gift of your

left life?' That line from a Carol Ann Duffy poem is playing in my head. If I plugged my head into the iPod speakers that's what I'd hear coming back at me.

The river is indifferent to Time but I am not. Big Ben chimes my life in quarter hours.

Thursday 23rd. There is a new moon. Like another chance. If I could just unmoor this boat.

3.30 a.m. There's a boat outside near the Festival Pier. I hope it's legal. There is CCTV everywhere. I am not the only one watching. A friend of mine had wanted to drop me at the pier to meet my berthed boat. Her own boat is small and jaunty but the rules have changed and Transport for London controls the pier. They wouldn't let us land. We are going to have to have an Occupy movement for everything soon.

4.10 a.m. Bridge. A woman with an orange suitcase waiting for the night bus.

Below. They have got into the railed-off area directly below the ship to have sex. She is reluctant. He is eager. He pulls her over the stacked metal towards the thrown piles of timber. He is undoing his trousers. She hasn't unbuttoned her coat.

4.17 a.m. The bus comes.

4.21 a.m. The couple reappears. He doesn't take her hand.

The boat is not quiet. In the day it has a splendid solitariness. At night the noises of London bounce off the concrete of the South Bank and the National Theatre. I live in the deep country not in the city. My hearing is good and I can hear all the separate sounds of the not-asleep city. I am like Roderick Usher in Poe's terrible story.

I am like the Lady of Shalott too. I sit in the window watching and no one sees me. I can't communicate with anyone – and I realize that even if I saw something terrible there is nothing I could do in time. It takes eight minutes to reach where I can see. That is about the same time as light takes to travel from the Sun to the Earth.

The distance from the Sun to the Earth is about 150,000 miles.

About dawn I fell asleep. I woke to a grey morning and the sound of scaffolding and disc saws. They are working below – where the couple had sex.

An ice-cream van has arrived under the window. Britain is the land of bad timing. The sunshine was yesterday. Today the little Lowry-like figures on the bridge have their hoods up again. The Battle of Britain. Wind. Rain. Grey.

Unmoor this boat – we can go …

Downriver like Elizabeth I setting off to greet Sir Francis Drake coming home with Spanish treasure. Downriver like Elizabeth II in her diamond flotilla; 1,000 boats they say will fill the Thames from all over the world.

I walked out at low tide this morning. When the tide is high life flows smoothly over memory and history. History is a collection of found objects washed up through time. Goods, ideas, personalities surface towards us then sink away. Some we hook out, others we ignore, and as the pattern changes, so does the meaning. We cannot rely on the facts. Time, that returns everything, changes everything.

A fridge door. A shopping trolley. Smashed-up skateboards. Oyster shells. There's a clay pipe and a billiard ball. A bundle of abandoned clothes. The end of one identity the beginning of another.

Mistah Kurtz — he dead.

Explanations drain away. History is a madman's museum. I think I understand what I see, but what I see is subject to the tide.

Unmoor the boat. Part miracle, part madness. My life is a series of set-sails and shipwrecks. I run aground, I cut loose. The rim is dangerously near the waterline. I feel like a saint in a coracle. Head thrown back. Sun on my throat.

Unmoor the boat.

Sven Lindqvist

Bed and Breakfast

The Tang dynasty painter Wu Tao-tzu one day stood looking at a mural he had just finished. Suddenly, he clapped his hands and the temple gates in the picture opened. He entered into his work, the gates closed behind him and he was never seen again.

When I first heard this tale as a child, entering a picture seemed a very natural thing to do. What else *could* you do?

Not to enter would have been to miss a golden opportunity. Pictures were few and far between in the 1930s, remember!

In Sweden there was in those days not a single television channel, no lush colour photographs in illustrated magazines, no coffee-table books full of eye-goodies, and very few children's books.

So when I saw a picture that was more than a black smudge on the page, I jumped at it. Or rather, I jumped *into* it, as if it was a jungle to explore or a room to live in.

The pictures that most excited my fantasy were often those on tins. Tins of sardines, of meat or even of tropical fruit.

Opening the tin was opening the picture.

Smelling the contents brought me to the brink of the picture world.

Eating was entering.

As a schoolboy, a few years later, I had already lost this natural gift of entering into pictures. I now took what seemed to me a more realistic view of the matter. I prepared myself for a career as a practising magician.

An older friend who was a professional and gave regular paid performances, showed me how some of his tricks were done. I used all my pocket money to buy a cloak, a wand and a top hat full of secret pockets.

Now when I heard the tale of Wu Tao-tzu my question was: *how did he do it*?

What was the secret behind the opening of the gates at the sound of clapping hands?

How did he manage the art of his own disappearance?

He seemed to have penetrated his painting and found an inner room, a liveable, habitable inner space, behind the surface of art. How was this illusion created?

Or was it, perhaps, not just an illusion? After all, the great German novelist Hermann Hesse spent his whole writing life trying to enact the myth of Wu Tao-tzu. Musil and Proust were not far behind.

The more I studied the myth of Wu Tao-tzu, the more I was fascinated by the possibilities it opened up.

Questions multiplied.

Why did he disap-pear?

What company did he leave behind?

Did he experience the culture of his day as desperate and meaningless?

Or was his vanishing rather an act of artistic self-confidence? An attempt, perhaps, to verify art in life?

Wu Tao-tzu had the courage for solitude. That is what is so tempting about his fate. He had the courage to disappear and continue alone, on the other side of the visible in art.

★

I have been on the lookout for Wu Tao-tsu all my life. I chased him in China, in India, in Africa. On my last long journey I found his tracks in the deserts of central Australia.

Few deserts are so well taken care of as the Australian. Every stone, every bush, every waterhole has its specific owner and custodian, its sacred history and religious significance. Every holy place has its own holy picture.

The eternal truths of Aboriginal religion are expressed in the surrounding landscape. The landscape is mapped in the holy picture. Pictures and places have a peculiar personal intimacy. You belong to them more than they belong to you.

It is your duty to travel to these places. To care for them. To paint the ground with the very pictures that map the ground.

You enter these pictures by painting your body with them. You enter them by dancing them back into the ground. You enter these pictures by dreaming them, by going to sleep in them, and sometimes even becoming pregnant by them. You survive by keeping these pictures alive. And by keeping them alive you do your bit to make the whole universe survive.

I write this from the roof of Queen Elizabeth Hall, looking out over the City, St Paul's and what was once London's East End. I am sitting in 'A Room for London', a project sponsored by an organization, Living Architecture, dedicated to the message that modern radical architecture is not only to be looked at from the outside. You can enter these houses and live in them.

So this is a room the Chinese painter Wu Tao-tzu could have entered after having clapped his hands.

It is a fully equipped bed and breakfast where he could have stayed the night.

It is even a room he could have lived in, if he wanted to leave the world. Who would have come looking for him on top of the Queen Elizabeth Hall?

Down below is London, dark, glittering, full of mysteries.

I first got to know London through *Jack* London. It seemed utterly significant to me that the man who explored the abyss of London had the same name as the city whose misery he uncovered. That couldn't be just a coincidence, could it? I was only nine years old and anything was possible then.

Jack London's *The People of the Abyss* was one of the first 'real' books I read.

It was 'real' in the sense that it was not a fairy tale for children or an adventure story made up for boys. The Abyss really existed. Jack London had been there. He had resisted all the authorities who had said that it was impossible to go to the East End and still more impossible to stay there.

'To live there yourself,' his friends said, disapprovingly. 'It can't be done, you know.'

Cook's travel agency would unhesitatingly and instantly have sent him to Darkest Africa or innermost Tibet, but to the East End of London, barely a stone's throw distant from Ludgate Circus, they knew not the way!

Finally, having burnt his boats behind him, he plunged alone into that human wilderness of which nobody seemed to know anything.

I came in secretly behind him.

'Nowhere in the streets of London may one escape the sight of abject poverty', said Jack.

It must not be forgotten that the summer of 1902 was considered 'good times' in England. The starvation and lack of shelter I encountered constituted a chronic condition of misery which is never wiped out, even in the periods of greatest prosperity.

Following the summer of 1902 came a hard winter. Great numbers of the unemployed formed into processions, as many as a dozen at a time, and daily marched through the streets of London crying for bread.

That I had never seen in Stockholm. I had never seen 'tottery old men and women searching in the garbage for rotten potatoes, beans, and vegetables'. During the unemployment of the 1930s hungry men often came to our door asking for 'a boiled potato'. Always that same boiled potato. It was the proper, simple, humble thing to ask for. It was the proper, simple, humble thing to give. You could not refuse a hungry man his boiled potato. Poverty and unemployment had this utmost boundary: the right not to the rotten, but to the boiled potato.

As a child I could always spot a child from a poor family. For one thing, they wore a particular type of mittens that came in the church's Christmas charity parcel.

They also had a peculiar smell. Most Swedish working-class families in those days lived in one-room apartments, with neither shower nor bathroom. So their children smelt of sweat and mould, of damp and dirt and overcrowding.

That was child poverty as I recognized it. But Jack London had seen 'little children clustered like flies around a festering mass of fruit, thrusting their arms to the shoulders into the liquid corruption, and drawing forth morsels but partially decayed, which they devoured on the spot'.

And their parents? What did their mothers say?

'The women from whose rotten loins they spring were everywhere,' wrote Jack London.

> They whined insolently, and in maudlin tones begged me for pennies, and worse. They held carouse in every boozing ken, slatternly, unkempt, bleary-eyed, leering and gibbering, overspilling with foulness and corruption, and, gone in debauch, sprawling across benches and bars, unspeakably repulsive, fearful to look upon.
>
> And I remember a lad of fourteen, and one of six or seven, white-faced and sickly, homeless, the pair of them, who sat upon the pavement with their backs against a railing and watched it all.

And watched it all.

I couldn't help feeling that Jack London used the child's perspective to paint an unfair picture of these women, yes, of all the people of the Abyss. Even so, Jack London's book made a great impression on me. When I finally visited England for the first time in 1948 what I wanted to see above all was the East End of London. I wanted to walk every street and enter every house mentioned in *The People of the Abyss*.

But they were all gone, bombed out. The abyss of war had obliterated the abyss of peace.

One of my early ambitions as a writer was to do a book about Wu Tao-tzu, using Jack London's method in *The People of the Abyss*.

His experiment had always fascinated me. It contained my own story. But I wanted to repeat it in a different direction – not descending into the abyss, but ascending into art.

Where did Wu Tao-tzu go when the gates in the mural opened? What did he do in there? What happened to him?

I can see it now. Literature has been really important to me only as Utopia.

In my books, and not only there
but also in the hopes I have,
in my demands on life,
in the motives of my actions,
briefly – everywhere it may have practical consequences.

I discover the same presumption as in Hesse, in Musil, in Proust.

As in the whole line of writers who have shaped me: that art is not closed to man, that man can step into art.

The opposite of the East End is not the West End. But where is it then? I want to know how people are living there and what they are living for. In short, I want to live there myself.

'Live there yourself?' said people with the most disapproving expressions. 'You can't, you know.'

It must be possible. The prospect of a clearer and freer way of living has always been held out to me in art and literature. It must exist. Somewhere.

I've seen it in poems and pictures. I've heard it in music. There's a fearlessness there that makes my life foolish.

There are opportunities for happiness there that frighten me more than unhappiness. There's an abyss in reverse and one falls upwards.

Why, then, do I live as I do?

Not even the professors at the university – scholarly men and women who without a moment's hesitation would have sent me to the darkest corners of the archives and the innermost petty details of the bibliographies – not even they could help me.

'Art as a way of living,' I tried to explain to them.

'Yes, of course! An excellent subject for a study of motifs.'

'But as a personal experiment?'

'What do you mean?'

'To examine the habitability of poetry. To live in a work of art.'

'Like you inhabit a house? You can't.'

'To test the ways of the spirit in practice.'

'That's – hmm – unprecedented. I don't think we can do anything for you.'

Clearly I had to manage on my own.

Having burnt my boats, I was now to enter a world about which no one seemed to know anything.

Like Jack London in 1902 in the city of the same name.

But in the opposite direction.

He stepped out of fiction, I wanted to enter.

He left his culture, I wanted to find the heart of mine.

I wanted to be present in the arts when they happen, an observer in disguise, an eyewitness of the spirit on the lookout for a better life than ours.

So I clapped my hands and started writing *The Myth of Wu Tao-tzu*. The first Swedish edition was published in 1967. It has never been out of print since then. The gates to the first English edition are now open. If you ever dreamed of a bed and breakfast in art, there is your chance.

★

As I was celebrating my eightieth birthday in a ship on the roof of the Queen Elizabeth Hall, my old friend, the Chinese painter Wu Tao-tzu, came to see me.

He liked the strangely beautiful piece of habitable art where I was staying.

But the problem that was bothering him now was not how to enter art and live there.

It was the problem of feeding ten billion people.

It was the problem of fuelling five billion motor cars.

It was the problem of building two billion houses and apartments.

Our consumption of oil, paper, meat, etc. cannot be multiplied by the population of the world. Natural resources would come to an end in a few decades, in some cases months.

The effects on the global climate would be disastrous.

We have created a lifestyle that makes injustice permanent and inescapable.

We have created a world where robots produce robots. Where capital breeds capital with very little need for the East-enders of the world.

Tell me what will happen when the majority of mankind has become technologically superfluous.

At the same time rebellious with hunger and economically unimportant.

What will then stop a final solution of the world problem?

In *The People of the Abyss* the Eastenders already saw it coming.

They are, Jack London wrote, 'encumbrances', of no use to anyone, not even to themselves. 'They clutter the earth with their presence and are better out of the way.'

The poor themselves felt there to be 'a wise mercy' in 'sending them over the divide'. In 1902, they already had a language for it. A dose of 'black jack' or 'white potion' would 'polish them off', they said. All agreed that the poor person who gave too much trouble would be quietly killed.

Jack London's East End was 'the world as I found it' in the first 'real' book of my young life.

At the heart of the world's darkness there was this quiet, peaceful genocide, accepted and agreed to even by those who were the next to be killed.

Caryl Phillips
A Bend in the River

Of course, it was T. S. Eliot who famously declared, 'April is the cruellest month,' and how right he was. Four days ago, soon after I ascended in the slow, slow, lift to the roof of the Queen Elizabeth Hall, it became clear that the weather would soon be taking a cruel turn. High winds and lashing rain one minute; the next a hint of blue sky, a slither of sunshine, and then back again to high winds and lashing rain. One was tempted to call it 'squally' weather. Another word which sprang to mind was 'marooned' – high above London, high above the Thames, looking down on Europe's largest city.

The first night was strangely eerie. It was a night punctuated by unfamiliar sounds. Screeching seagulls, wires stretching and singing, wood creaking and popping and snapping, the swishing backwash of water, and the occasional dull bass of a tugboat. And then the noises of the land; Big Ben counting off the hours, the dull hum of traffic on Waterloo Bridge, and garbage carts being noisily trundled across pavements below. And then I was rewarded with the drama of light crashing through the flimsy blinds and the dramatic announcement of a new day. I crawled out of bed and took in an extraordinary vista. An 180 degree view of London as she curves around the graceful bend in the river at the heart of the city.

It seems appropriate that I should have had T. S. Eliot in mind at the inception of my residency, for in many ways it is Eliot's vision of the Thames and the City of London that had been resonating most powerfully in my head when thinking of this short sojourn in the sky. In *The Waste Land*, Eliot – an American migrant to London – wrote memorably of the 'Unreal City' of London.

> Unreal City,
> Under the brown fog of a winter dawn,
> A crowd flowed over London Bridge, so many,
> I had not thought death had undone so many.

Hardly cheery words, but that foggy poetic image of London was, strangely enough, what I expected to be gazing down upon. I had anticipated endless lines of people shuffling across bridges to the left and to the right with, as Eliot suggests, each man fixing his eyes before his feet and silently going about his business. But that's not the London I saw before me from my elevated vantage point. The fog of the first half of the twentieth century has long gone, and I haven't detected much shuffling; in fact, people appear to dash purposefully in all directions. These Londoners don't look at all as though death has undone them. From the prow of my boat in the sky, exuberant and energetic London is clearly open for business and busy.

But preconceptions are powerful, and we often hold on to them long after reality has intervened. Between 1948 and 1962, over 250,000 West Indians arrived in Britain, British citizens clinging to suitcases, gaudy hats, and with their passports of belonging tucked neatly into their jacket pockets. They were coming to the motherland and their minds were full of images of the empire's most important city. Marble Arch. Buckingham Palace. Hyde Park Corner. The images were iconic, and knowledge of them suggested participation, a shared history. Possessing these images – being able to recognize these places and, most importantly, talk about them with the authority of an insider – would surely produce a happy encounter with Britain. These early West Indian migrants arrived in Britain holding on to their preconceptions as tightly as they held on to their luggage.

Over fifty years later, many of those original pioneer migrants are still living in London. We know what these migrants expected because their testimony is preserved in audio archives and in documentary films. We also know what they expected because of the literature of the period, and perhaps the most evocative, and brilliant, example of this literature is Samuel Selvon's novel *The Lonely Londoners*, first published in 1956. Selvon's main character, Moses Aloetta, finds himself, at the end of the novel, standing by the same river that I'm now perched high above. Despite the evidence of discrimination, poverty and heartbreak that Moses is forced to endure throughout the book, at the end of the novel our Lonely Londoner is unable to jettison his images of expectation. He stands gloriously still on the banks of the Thames knowing that he can't help but love this city that has effectively rejected him and his kind, and somewhat ironically he comforts himself by lovingly recollecting London's iconic images and locales:

> Oh … [he says] to have said: 'I walked on Waterloo Bridge,' 'I rendezvoused at Charing Cross,' 'Piccadilly Circus is my playground,' to say these things, to have lived these things, to have lived in the great city of London, centre of the world. To one day lean against

the wind walking up the Bayswater Road (destination unknown), to see the leaves swirl and dance and
spin on the pavement (sight unseeing), to write a
casual letter home beginning: 'Last night in Trafalgar
Square ...'

Selvon's characters grapple with the symbolism of iconic
London, and the protracted and frustrating nature of their
struggle suggests deep and unresolved issues around questions
of belonging and ownership in the Britain of the period. Landscapes are freighted with history and can suggest a national
identity; they can also remain stubbornly standoffish and hold
outsiders at bay.

For the past few days I have been witness to the silent muscular
power of the river flowing beneath me, history emerging from
its impenetrable depths. I have exchanged visions of Romans
sailing up the Thames for Conradian visions of ships at anchor
waiting for the fog to lift. I have contemplated contemporary
images of immigrants sailing up the river and disembarking at
Tilbury Docks, some way downriver to my right. I have also
looked out at the grandeur of the buildings: St Paul's Cathedral,
The Palace of Westminster, Somerset House, Waterloo Bridge,
at the whole spread of the most familiar landmarks of the city
laid out before me, and I've done so without feeling the same
clamour for ownership that Moses so desperately desired. And,
I might add, without feeling any of Eliot's gloomy ambivalence.

However, gazing upon these iconic buildings I *have* found
myself thinking, every minute of every day, about the enduring
power of British history, and how we continue to struggle to
distinguish the past from the present, the purely ceremonial

from the essential, in a way which might enable us to move forward as a modern nation. Fifty years on from lonely Moses on the banks of the Thames, I've not been thinking of, and hoping for, ownership. I've simply been musing on the vexing problems of how to make the narrative of our history, as evidenced in the landscape and buildings, fit with the narrative of a twenty-first-century, multicultural, multiracial, people. One would never want to dismiss the evidence of grandeur, achievement, and tradition suggested by this landscape. But questions remain that go beyond the symbolic; just how relevant is the role of an established church in British life? The role of the monarchy? The desirability of an unelected upper house? I scan to the left, and back to the right, and then look down at the people on the streets and there seems to be disjuncture between the narrative on the streets and the narrative suggested by this particular view.

Such questioning seems to me to be part of the legacy of growing up in the second half of the twentieth century, during the years in which Britain lost an empire and somewhat reluctantly began to reconfigure her sense of herself. These are the years in which Britain – kicking and screaming – became both multiracial and European. However, I had initially assumed that the writers of the first half of the twentieth century who grappled with these questions of identity and belonging under the full gaze of empire must have had a harder time of it than those of us in the post-empire world. But after these past few days up here in Mr Conrad's boat, I'm not so sure. Publicly questioning our history is a healthy development, but it remains nonetheless unnerving. However, doing so will lead us forward to a place where we might responsibly start to question the ever-changing criteria for membership of a nation – this nation – while remaining cognizant of the fact that there are among us, in early twenty-first-century Britain, countless numbers of Moses Aloettas, of all backgrounds, who are metaphorically standing on the banks of the Thames and simply dreaming of belonging.

On my second day atop the Queen Elizabeth Hall, I crossed the river and went to the Embankment where I sought out Yvonne, an elderly Caribbean person who, for the past seven years, has established some sort of a home for herself on the banks of the Thames. Smart, intelligent, not addicted to drugs or drink, she lives in and around Victoria Embankment Gardens near the seventeenth-century Watergate, which depicts the old water line of the Thames before the building of the Embank-ment. I found her on a bench, surrounded by a huge pile of bags and suitcases – in short, her worldly possessions. She was asleep on a bright Sunday morning and so I didn't disturb her. Instead, I continued to wander up and down the Thames, taking a closer look at these buildings which signify a particu-larly powerful history, contemplating both their symbolic, and actual, significance in 2012 in this culturally hybrid city of London.

I eventually wandered back to Mr Conrad's boat and sat out on deck and looked at the lights playing on the undulat-ing blanket of water, which bestowed upon it a glossy patina of melancholy. And then I took out my copy of *The Lonely Londoners* and read the first few lines again, feeling the unease and ambivalence in the words: 'One grim winter evening, when it had a kind of unrealness about London, with a fog sleeping restlessly over the city and the lights showing in the blur as if is not London at all but some strange place on another planet …'

That's it, exactly, I thought; 'some strange place on another planet …' For so many people the possibility of their participating in the type of Britain that these buildings symbolically suggest, remains for them about as real as the possibility of their participating in lunar exploration. It's not the fault of the buildings, of course, but it's what the buildings suggest. Exclusivity; privilege; power. Cumulatively the evidence of the buildings forms a powerful narrative that for many is a narrative of rejection. Even if one did take the time to learn the actual *and* symbolic meaning of this resplendent view of the city, the confident narrative at the heart of the city might well still neither recognize you, let alone embrace you and take you in.

The fact is, Britain's history as evident in the buildings along this particular stretch of river suggests a tradition that no longer really squares with the Britain that we deal with on a daily basis. Britain is no longer exclusively Judaeo-Christian. English is not the only language we hear daily on the streets. The monarchy is not universally respected. And the upper house of our parliament could use some serious reform.

Britain, like most European nations, is not particularly open to hyphenation. We don't talk easily of Jewish-Britons, or Afro-Britons, or Swedish-Britons, thus making it relatively easy to couple one's cultural traditions to national identity. Being British remains a largely concrete identity, quite well gated, and not particularly flexible. For the past four days I've gazed upon the most familiar and easily identifiable aspects of British identity, as evidenced in the buildings on this particular bend in the river, and wondered about the plight of those who wish to belong to this nation but feel, for whatever reasons, locked out by dint of nationality, gender, race, class or religion. And, of course, I've wondered about the situation of those who *have* belonged and then capitulated to some form of participation fatigue. The 7 July bombers, for instance. It seems clear that in our early twenty-first century the process of engaging with these vexing issues of British identity and exclusion has, if anything, become an increasingly urgent part of our social contract. Something which I feel would not have surprised either gloomy Eliot or tremulously anxious Selvon.

From the vantage point of my boat here on top of the Queen Elizabeth Hall on the South Bank of the river, I am witnessing iconic London; iconic Britain. What I'm gazing upon is the familiar, hugely exportable, and in a sense, very comfortable, public face of Britain. Soon after my arrival on the boat, the suggestive rootedness, and unselfreflective confidence of these buildings – for instance the self-conscious grandeur of the Savoy Hotel directly across the river – began to irritate me. Yesterday I finally gave up and jumped on a Thames Clipper and headed off downriver in search of another vision of London. And of course, I found it. The historic buildings of Bankside and Shakespeare's Globe gave way to the Tower of London, and then to the astonishing array of modern flats around the newly revamped Isle of Dogs. The Dubai-like spectacle of Canary Wharf appears almost like a mirage, and beyond this there is the glory of Greenwich Palace and then the extraterrestrial vision of the O2 arena. And beyond this? Well, less development and a reminder of an earlier unregenerated Thames. I went in search of other visions of London and found many Londons which, on my return to my own little rooftop boat, made me feel slightly more comfortable with my iconically powerful view. After all, it's just a view, right? One which carries the authority and weight of power, but is no more representative of London than the Isle of Dogs or the underdeveloped wastelands beyond Greenwich. But tell that to the tourists. Or to Moses Aloetta standing motionless on the banks of the Thames and wanting to belong – to belong to *this* London on my gentle bend in the river, not those Londons to the east. To the idea of London and Britain that constitutes my view. Can it really be true that not all views are equal? And if this is the case, is it possible, or even desirable, to make the narrative embedded in the view of London that is spread out before me available to everybody in Britain? Not for the first time I'm glad that Mr Conrad's boat has come equipped with window blinds.

MAY

Maya Jasanoff
A River Passage

From my bed ringed by ten windows I scarcely see the Thames, but the city unfolds from St Paul's to Westminster, the river held in the arms of church and state. Most anywhere else, a box of windows on a roof would be a watchtower – and this could be a voyeur's paradise. It comes equipped with two sets of binoculars. The weather has been glorious, and in just three days of looking at the people flowing below, I've seen a summer's-worth of limbs and bellies bared to the sun. But sitting on 'deck', the London Eye circling deliberately over me, I'm the most exposed: the odd woman out, on a ledge.

I've discovered that nowhere from my eyrie can I frame a photograph of the river naked, with no human trace. The nearest I get is a band of water with the pom-pom tops of two trees bobbing into the shot. It's mud-brown – the kind of brown that can't be redeemed by warmer words, like nutmeg or terracotta, that summon the baked or the spiced. It winks at the sun as if it were an old roué who's gotten a rare chance to flirt.

The Thames in London is less a river of nature than of nurture, bent and banked to the needs of a commercial city. It's been a hard-working river, bolstered by huge networks of nineteenth-century docks, built to hold the wealth of nations. It has witnessed devastation, as during the Great Fire, when thousands of Londoners hurled themselves into the Thames for safety – or the Blitz, when the docks became honey to the bombers. And it's been a jolly river, too, of pubs, pleasure gardens, and people messing about in boats – a river of spectacles and pageants.

Two days from now, a thousand boats will fill this stretch of water to celebrate Queen Elizabeth II's Diamond Jubilee. I've seen it coming: barricades clanged into place along Waterloo Bridge, pennants strung over Charing Cross station, patrol boats slicing under Hungerford Bridge. Think *Gloriana*, the flotilla insists, for this, too, is an Elizabethan age.

But in the sixteenth century, any day you looked there were two thousand boats on London's river; and by Queen Victoria's Diamond Jubilee, there were five thousand sailboats and six thousand steamers registered on the Thames, together with oil tanks to fuel them, vast basins to hold them, warehouses to store their goods – and tens of thousands of labourers to service them. Ordinary Londoners chatted in terms owned by experts now; they recognized hoys, shallops, lighters, cutters, colliers, clinkers, ferries and wherries, as clearly as you distinguish Ryanair from BA. Now a thousand boats have become a marvel – while London Terminal Control manages more than four thousand flights per day.

The first so-called river I knew was also an urban river, the East River in New York – which sadly isn't even a river but a strait, dividing Manhattan from Long Island. My grandparents lived in a high-rise apartment complex called Waterside Plaza, which was as close to the river as it sounds. You could take an elevator to the bottom level of their building and step straight out on to a riverbank boardwalk, which my grandfather methodically paced for exercise. I'd trot ahead, past *Miami Vice*-style yachts, and up to the 34th Street Heliport, where I'd stand against the chain-link fence with fingers in my ears, hair flying, to watch the helicopters lift and drop. (In a fit of casual extravagance, my aunt once took me and my brother up for a heart-swelling swirl over Manhattan, which still counts – adjusting for age – as one of the most exhilarating things I've ever done.)

Under the cracks in the boardwalk and around the slime-coated wooden posts lapped the river, with latherings of foam, clots of detritus, objects lost and tossed, clumps of feathers connoting avian tragedy. For a long time, I thought this was how real water, wild water, was meant to smell: briny and fishy, with a metallic finish that clapped your nose, a smell that grew richer and creamier the hotter it got.

One day on his walk by the East River, my grandfather had a stroke and dropped dead. He had been born in probably the most river-laced land in the world, what's now Bangladesh, so there was justice in dying next to a river too (even if it's really a strait). In a later season, our family went to an uptown stretch of the East River, by Gracie Mansion, and leaned over a railing to let his ashes out of the bag, over the water, the way Hindus traditionally do. It was the right end in the wrong river.

Thinking of the sacred rivers of India, T. S. Eliot wrote: 'I do not know much about gods; but I think that the river/ Is a strong, brown god – sullen, untamed and intractable.'

What power do rivers wield? Rivers thread, line, cut, or snake and lattice through landscapes. They run, they rush, they fall – they rise, flood and course. Rivers can be bridged, forded, dammed, covered over and tunnelled beneath. Rivers have beginnings and ends, sources and mouths. They have currents, direction, and, by implication, purpose. The metaphors they invite concern time, volume, and trajectories: rivers of life and death, rivers of blood, gold, tears and sorrows, rivers of dreams, history, and faith.

When you travel by river, you are either going up or coming down. It's quite different when you journey by sea. Seas stretch and spread beyond visible bounds; they have shores, not banks; they're wide, not long. 'The river is within us, the sea is around us,' says Eliot. Seas have waves, swells, and tides. They're moody and consuming: they buffet, heave, toss and swallow. While river-time is linear, spanning the past and the future, time at sea is circular, orbital, defined by the moon and stars. While on rivers you travel with or against the current, at sea you are – well, at sea. You can think you're heading for China and find yourself in Cuba; you can set course for Virginia and wash up in Massachusetts. Seas speak of freedom: rife with dangers, rich with possibilities.

Stories about rivers and stories about seas (or at least, the European and American ones that I know best) each have certain distinctive features. Stories about rivers often involve passages from an exterior to an interior, and a search for something hidden, something rumoured: concealed treasure, secret passages, disguised points of origin or egress. Some of the best-known river stories happen to be histories, and true – like that of Walter Raleigh questing for El Dorado on the Orinoco; or René Caillié struggling up the Niger to Timbuktu; or Livingstone, Burton, and the rest, looking for the source of the Nile.

You can follow a river *into* something, but you always put *out* to sea. Sea stories dramatize a tension between the contained and the infinite: the enclosed shipmates afloat on an ocean, the castaway on an island, the one true star that guides the way. A ship in a sea is a ship in a bottle. In sea stories, things aren't so much hidden as they are simply unknown and open-ended. Where will we land? What shall we find? At sea you're much more likely than on a river to run into creatures with three heads, or six arms, or one eye. It's by sea that you'll find Scylla and Charybdis, the Houyhnhnms, and the Great White Whale. The sea invites fantasy, marvel, and the unexpected, which may be why the best-known sea stories are fiction.

When Joseph Conrad joined the British merchant marine in the 1870s, Europeans had charted the coastlines that had eluded them just a century or two before. Nobody any longer rendered California as an island, or left off the western half of Australia. Indeed, sea coasts were more prosperous and populous than ever. Before 1800, the great world capitals – Rome, Cairo, Beijing, Mexico City – lay inland, safe from marauders, fed by hinterlands. Many of today's megacities, by contrast – Rio, Lagos, Calcutta, Hong Kong – sit on coasts, where Europeans decided to put them. By Conrad's time, imperialism and industrialization had tamed seas into highways – while the great mysteries lay inland.

Conrad spent twenty years as a merchant sailor, almost entirely on British ocean-going ships. He made numerous passages to Singapore and Australia and spent almost two years at a stretch cruising around Siam and the Dutch East Indies, particularly Borneo. Conrad's last command (though he didn't plan it that way), in 1890, was a six-week stint on the *Roi des Belges*, a steamer plying the Congo River in the vast swathe of central Africa that was run as a personal colonial fiefdom by

King Leopold II of Belgium. Set against the rest of his maritime career, Conrad's Congo journey was brief, anomalous, and unforgettable. He saw first-hand some of the outrages that made Leopold's Congo Free State into a synonym for slaughter and abuse. It was, in every way, a very bad trip.

When Conrad began writing fiction – at about the time he travelled to Congo – he worked with what he knew best: he wrote of the sea, of Borneo, and, in his words, 'human outcasts such as one finds in the lost corners of the world'. But he loathed being classified as a writer of sea stories. Twelve years after publishing his first novel, he at last wrote a book without boats. 'I have just finished a novel (?) with not a drop of water in it – except the rain, which is quite natural since everything takes place in London,' he announced. It was called *The Secret Agent*, and would, he hoped, shatter 'preconceived notions of Conrad as sea writer'.

I wonder what Conrad would have made of the fact that, a century later, he's remembered less for any of these books than for just one early work: *Heart of Darkness*. Like the Congo journey that inspired it, the novella is brief, anomalous, and unforgettable. Brief enough to be written in six weeks over a Christmas holiday. Anomalous because Conrad's imagination, otherwise, was deep in Borneo, where he set the books he was writing before and after *Heart of Darkness*, and where Marlow made his next appearance, in *Lord Jim*.

And unforgettable because … ? The power of *Heart of Darkness* resides in its breaking – and blending – of conventions. For Conrad's great achievement in *Heart of Darkness* is to write the quintessential river story by making it also, in some sense, a story of the sea. The beginning unfolds in an estuary, where river and sea meet. It's told on the deck of a sailing yacht, by a mariner who still 'followed the sea'. Its language mixes oceanic metaphors of mystery and the infinite with a riverine awareness of lineages and secrets. It turns a classic river passage from an exterior to an interior into the seaman's nightmare of drifting in a limitless expanse of horror. What starts as a search for sources becomes a search for monsters.

That's why, in Conrad's vision, all rivers begin to flow into one another – just as the seas do. The rivers of Borneo, which Conrad knew best, run in his imagination into the Congo. The Congo runs into the Thames. In other hands, the Congo will run into the Mekong, and the Amazon. After Conrad, any river can come to a bad end.

On my last day aboard this version of the *Roi des Belges* – a boat run aground on a roof, how's that for an unforgettable anomaly? – clouds blinded the sun, rain flicked the windows. The outlook for the *Reine de la Grande Bretagne*'s pageant wasn't too bright. But enough with the outlook, I thought: I had to get out and about. I walked to Greenwich, past signs of prosperity blighted and renewed, survivals and excavations. At Rotherhithe, passing one of the riverside stairs – a London *ghat* – a sound stopped me short. It slurped and chuckled. It was the tide of the river, licking the muddy bank. It was, unmistakeably, the sound of the sea.

JUNE

Michael Ondaatje
A Port Accent

As a boy, between the ages of eleven and eighteen, I crossed the Thames every day on my way to school in South London. And during the summers, for two years, I had a job at Battersea Fun Fair, over there on the South Bank, working in the Forte's restaurant and in one of their booths near the Big Dipper. So this river was a constant in my new life in England, though at that time we were living in Fulham, rather than here, where I am now, in this re-creation of Conrad's fictional steamer, over-looking the very heart of London's power and wealth.

Then a few years ago a friend took me on his skiff along the Thames. We went east towards the Thames estuary so I could once again see the Tilbury Docks where I had landed from a ship in the 1950s, a boy from Sri Lanka, in order to go to school in England. I was in the middle of researching that journey and my arrival in England. And that afternoon, coming upon it by boat from the city on a rainy afternoon, Tilbury looked a small, insignificant, unpainted place. It had none of the grandeur I imagined it should have, as the 'Entrance to England' for so many visitors and immigrants, though I realize in retrospect that 'gateways' to great countries often downplay their wealth. Immigrants to Canada arriving in Halifax had to walk almost a mile in order to formally 'enter' the country. It seemed an inten-tional humiliation. Now, as we drifted a mile or so from Tilbury, large ships seemed to be grazing in the distance, preparing to dock. They were most likely container ships, my friend told me, rather than passenger ships from Asia. In any case, when I came to write about my arrival at Tilbury as a boy, this outing led me to describe it as an undramatic event:

We slipped into England in the dark. After all our weeks at sea, we were unable to witness our entrance into the country. Just a pilot barge, blinking its blue light, was waiting at the entrance of the estuary, and guided us alongside a dark unknown shoreline into the Thames.

There was the sudden smell of land. When the dawn eventually lit whatever was around us, it seemed a humble place. We saw no green river banks or famous cities or great spanning bridges that might open up their two arcs to let us through. Everything we were passing seemed a remnant from another industrial time — jetties, saltings, the entrances to dredged channels. We passed tankers and mooring buoys. We searched for the heraldic ruins we had learned about a thousand miles away in a history class in Colombo. We saw a spire. Then suddenly we were in a place full of names: South End, Chapman, Blythe Sands, Lower Hope, Shorn Mead.

Our ship gave four short blasts, there was a pause, then another blast, and we began to angle gently against the dock at Tilbury. *The Oronsay*, that had been for weeks like a great order around us, finally rested. Further upriver, deeper inland in this eastern cut of the Thames, were Greenwich, and Henley. But we had stopped now, finished with engines.

After all the vast seas here was a small unpainted terminal building on the Thames.

Tilbury now feels like a name lost to history, but this was where so many landed – coming from Asia, Australia, the Caribbean, the Mediterranean and Europe. Gandhi arrived here in 1888 (two years after the docks were built); Tagore in 1912; Sam Selvon in the 1950s. Józef Korzeniowski arrived in England in 1878, barely knowing anyone for fifteen years until he met Edward Garnett in 1894, and changed his name to Joseph Conrad. He too lived for years in solitude, a 'lonely Londoner', speaking with the heavy foreign accent he would retain all his life.

After an hour or so, my friend and I began the twenty-five mile journey on the skiff from this deserted industrial zone back to the centre of London. In two hours we were looking up at a grander planet. The Palace of Westminster, Tower Bridge, Victoria Tower, etc., etc. 'And this also' (as Conrad's Marlow announces suddenly in *Heart of Darkness*) 'has been one of the dark places of the earth.'

We are never told what books Marlow reads. It feels to us as if all his knowledge of human nature comes from meeting people and from the geographical and social realities he witnesses on his journeys. One assumes Marlow reads, of course; he appears to be a literate man, he has a good turn of phrase. Yet in the end what *frees* Conrad's books is the strange, complete lack of reference to any literary or artistic or even specific political allusions of a particular time. No Maupassant, not Flaubert's historical novel *Salammbo* that Conrad had studied carefully as a writer, not even his contemporary Henry James – books which Marlow could have lost himself in when abandoned on those long nights at sea or in some foreign port. What *did* Marlow do during those evenings? Was he just listening to

others? Or fine-tuning and then retelling those potent anec-
dotes about lives he'd witnessed?

Someone once mentioned the phrase 'port accents' to me.
And the idea of the existence of such a thing hovered in the
air while I was writing my novel about a sea journey. Now
and then the ship I was writing about would dock at Aden
or Port Said, and the talk in those ports would be not so
much the language of the country but a language based on
commerce and transport. It would be speedy and efficient,
a casually invented, informal Esperanto, a lingo that did not
involve translation so much as a crashing together of nouns and
phrases like the commentaries during hockey games in Canada
that include Quebec *joual* as well as English colloquialisms; a
useful but non-existent language, a 'connecting' language, the
word 'pidgin' deriving from the old Chinese pronunciation of
the English word for 'business'; a language that came into being
as a result of sailors communicating with those living on coasts,
or along some river delta, or the Amazon. (Speaking of which
– and I have always wanted to interrupt myself, Marlow-like –
one of the great books on river journeys is *Gerontius* by James
Hamilton Paterson: a novel about the real-life voyage up the
Amazon taken by Elgar in his old age.)

A port accent, then, is language at the far end of the scale
from Henry James. And you always imagine you are witnessing it in Conrad, who spent years trolling and loitering in the
distant coasts of the Far East before eventually coming up the
Thames and slipping into the canon of English literature as an
unlikely adopted son.

But in fact we *never* witness that port language and dialogue
in his work. We hear it referred to in *Youth*, where the ship,

waiting to take off on the south coast of England, is mocked by other crews, or among the disgraced sailors preparing for trial in god knows what distant place. We feel we have spent all our time with the ship chandlers along harbour streets and reclamation roads. But in fact all those voices are only distilled through the language of Marlow, never actually given to us. He is our translator, but also our obstacle, someone who gets in the way of all that local communion.

Marlow! This rational but intuitive Englishman invented by a Polish sea captain, who sits safely on a boat on the Thames interpreting for us all those journeys he took into the far-flung world.

The Thames, that now seems so individual and iconic and monolithic, had, according to Peter Ackroyd and other historians of this river, a hundred tributaries in earlier times: the Churn, the Windrush, the Kennet, the Wey, the Mole and many others. And there were even more streams that modestly entered and 'refreshed' the great river – Ampney Brook, Gatwick Stream, Hole Bourne, the Fleet (just below Blackfriars Bridge), and Barking Creek. Nearly all of them are now buried.

Ackroyd also lists the numerous professions along the Thames that in medieval times covered almost every yard of riverbank: customs officers, hook fishermen, conservators of embankments and weirs, water bailiffs, tide-men, draymen, laundresses, marine-store keepers, oystermen, toll keepers – something like two thousand people worked on this river in the 1700s. Dredgers would search for property that had fallen overboard. 'Mud larks' would hunt along the shores at low tide for stray pieces of coal. (And we suddenly remember that great opening chapter in *Our Mutual Friend* where a body is pulled out of the river and Dickens' plot begins.)

But if we go even further back to a much earlier book – to 54 BC – we find Julius Caesar writing in *The Gallic Wars*, 'how, greatly alarmed by the Roman arrival, the Britons placed Cassivellaunus over the whole conduct of the war'. Caesar describes how 'all the Britons dye themselves with woad, which occasions a bluish colour, and thereby have a terrible appearance in fight. They wear their hair long, and have every part of their body shaved except their head and upper lip. Ten and even twelve have wives common to them, and particularly brothers among brothers, and parents among their children.'

From Caesar to Franklin to Lewis and Clark to Darwin, there's this long tradition of writing about military or commercial or scientific journeys across seas and up great rivers, travelling, as one early explorer in South America claimed to have done, 'with my soul between my teeth'. And, as has been pointed out, from 1880 until the 1920s there was a passion among readers in England for adventurous travel fiction – *King Solomon's Mines*, *The Lost World*, *Tarzan of the Apes*, *The Time Machine*. So we need to place Conrad's *Heart of Darkness* in the midst of such popular adventures, in order to recognize how different it was and still is.

But in fact most voyages by sea were more benign. Gandhi, for instance, published a journal that he wrote on his 1888 trip to England in a magazine called *The Vegetarian*. It's a tender recollection, remembering how he lived on the sweetmeats and fruit he had brought on board with him, and how he would play the ship's piano. He found the arrangements of the water closets astonishing: 'We do not get water there, and are obliged to use pieces of paper.' When the ship reached Plymouth he saw nothing but fog. Twenty-four hours later the passengers 'reached Tilbury, left the steamer and arrived at the Victoria Hotel in London on the 27th October, at 4 p.m.'

On his return to India he is quite sentimental about his attachment to London: 'Who would not be – London with its teaching institutions, public galleries, museums, theatres, and public parks is a fit place for a student and a traveller.'

Gandhi continues:

> How did the vegetarians manage in the ship? Well, there were only two vegetarians, including myself ... Now I thought it was time for me to poke my nose in. I requested the secretary of the committee who managed these things to give me a quarter of an hour for a short speech on Vegetarianism. The secretary obligingly nodded consent to my request.
>
> Well I made grand preparations ... I well knew that I had to meet a hostile audience. The secretary had asked me to be humorous. I told him that I might be nervous, but humorous I could not be.

Gandhi would always be in the best of spirits on his various sea journeys. It is said he 'rode the pitching seas like a veteran mariner, and selected for himself a corner on the second-class deck where he spent most of the day and the whole of the night under the canopy of the starlit sky'.

But a few years later, in 1909, on a journey from London to Cape Town – it was a fifteen-day journey by ship – Gandhi was overcome by a desire to write a book, called *Hind Swaraj*, that formulated a plan for Indian Independence. It was to be his first book, and the writing of it is one of the great stories of *any* book being written at sea.

> The obsession was so great that he began writing on the ship stationery with a pencil. The thoughts were coming so furiously that he could not stop writing. When his right hand began to ache, he switched to writing with his left. The book was completed before he reached Cape Town.

How one would like to get hold of that manuscript and compare the arguments presented by the left hand and the right hand! (His left-hand writing was apparently more legible.) In any case this switching of hands became a habit all his life. Sometimes, under heavy pressure of work, he wrote on 'running trains'. And again when his right hand got tired, he wrote with the left. Some of his famous editorials bore the mark 'On the train'.

Another writer, Rabindranath Tagore, would also make a crucial journey from India to England by ship in 1912. And what Tagore wrote on his first journey to England would completely change his life. He spent the whole journey translating and reworking his Bengali poems from *Gitanjali*. And it was this manuscript, lionized by Yeats and other English poets shortly afterwards, that led to his being given the Nobel Prize.

> Now when I was a little chap I had a passion for maps. I would look for hours at South America, or Africa, or Australia, and lose myself in all the glories

of exploration. At that time there were many blank spaces on the earth, and when I saw one that looked particularly inviting ... I would put my finger on it and say, 'When I grow up I will go there.'

This is one of the famous paragraphs in Joseph Conrad's *Heart of Darkness*. Later, as an adult, his narrator, Marlow, will return to the map of Africa:

True, by this time it was not a blank space any more. It had got filled since my boyhood with rivers and lakes and names ... It had become a place of darkness. But there was in it one river especially, a mighty big river, that you could see on the map, resembling an immense snake uncoiled, with its head in the sea ... Then I remembered there was a big concern, a Company for trade on that river ...

A map clarifies in a glance where the power lies. It shows you immediately what the political perspective of the geographer is, just as we can interpret everything in that paragraph of Marlow's – the assumption that the filled-in space must be 'a place of darkness', and the lack of comment concerning the inherent and about-to-pounce desire and power of the 'Company', with its *interest* in that river. It reflects the wise remark, 'To have a great Language, you first of all must have a great Navy.' In a wonderful book called *Lords of the Sea*, John R. Hale demonstrates how the Athenian Navy was able completely to alter history in the Mediterranean, not just in terms of political force, but also by altering and spreading democracy and culture, and so becoming the hub and control of all forms of scientific knowledge and trade across that inland sea.

In any case, whenever we look down upon a map, the place in the centre at the base of the map is where power is located. We look at North America and automatically are used to seeing Canada far away to the north, in the less important distance. Marlow looks at a map of Africa and sees the white space far away, and so concludes whatever is there is thus not as significant. We look at the map of Sri Lanka, and Colombo will be at the centre, at the horizon line of our gaze, while far into the north is Jaffna.

A remarkable new work by T. Shanaathanan, called *The Incomplete Thombu*, startlingly begins with an almost unrecognizable map of Sri Lanka – until you realize it is *upside down* (with place names and towns printed the right way up). So Point Pedro and Keerimalai and Kodikaman are at our natural eye level, while the southern part of the island, where the power and the narrative voice usually reside, is now somewhere to the distant north, and in fact not even on the map – it is offstage. The furthest north, or 'south', we get is Vavuniya.

Winslow's Tamil dictionary defines a *thombu* as a public register of lands – it is a word not used in any country outside Sri Lanka. (How many such words were there, with a precise local meaning, along those river banks that Caesar and Speke and Burton and Marlow travelled past and gazed at from their boats?)

What we have in a book like *The Incomplete Thombu* is not a passing glance at a place, but an intimate documenting of properties and lands belonging to Tamil-speaking people prior to 'single or multiple displacements' from their homes in the north of Sri Lanka between 1983 and 2009. The data provided is direct and simple: first there's an informal drawing by the displaced occupant of what he remembers of the property and where things had been – a well, a fence, a palmyrah tree, an office. This is followed by an architectural drawing of the same site based on that informal sketch. Then a quietly devastating statement by the owners of how the property was lost. And then a drawing by the artist based on an image from that statement.

But it is T. Shanaathanan's re-invented and re-aligned map at the start of his book that prepares the reader and viewer for this new perspective in order to discover what has really taken place here, in the distant Jaffna Peninsula, a land of no rivers, just salt-water lagoons, and a surrounding sea.

I mentioned earlier the lack of reference to art and literary works in Conrad's writing. It's as if he did not want to limit himself to the time period he was in, in order to give a universal fable-like quality to his novels. So there is an unmirrored and unaesthetic rawness of event and character in his work. And this, of course, is also the political problem in a work like *Heart of Darkness*.

King Leopold of Belgium's forced-labour policies in the Congo killed over ten million people in that one territory, and between 1902 and 1913 this was known worldwide as *the* major atrocity of that era. Adam Hochschild in his book *King Leopold's Ghost* speaks of all this, and points out that Conrad's novella does *not* mention Leopold, *or* the Congo, or even Africa. The story, therefore, while being permanently universal is also permanently evasive. But Hochschild says that Conrad still revealed the basic moral issue of race and imperialism. 'He perceived,' Hochschild says, 'more than he knew.' Whatever Conrad subliminally revealed of himself in the novella, the slim book he wrote is a stake in the heart, unforgotten, unforgiven.

And yet, whatever appals us about Conrad's subconscious racism in *Heart of Darkness* (and this was an absolute product of his age), when Marlow turns suddenly to his listeners on the boat on the Thames, and says, 'And this also has been one of the dark places of the earth … I was thinking of very old times, when the Romans first came here, nineteen hundred years ago – the other day …', he is also twisting around the map of perspective. It is hardly surprising that one of the passengers on the boat responds to his remark with, 'Try to be civil.'

The light rain was still falling that late afternoon in Tilbury, as my friend's shallow skiff continued to make its way west towards the city. We stopped for a while at the Pelican Stairs for a snack, and then went on. The sun set; the dusk fell on the stream, and lights began to appear along the shore. And farther west on the upper reaches the place of the monstrous town was still marked ominously on the sky, a brooding gloom in sunshine, a lurid glare under the stars. '"And this also," said Marlow suddenly, "has been one of the dark places of the earth."'

I arrived just a few days ago and climbed up into this 'steam-ship' perched above the Thames. An English rain fell all night on the *Roi des Belges*. I had brought a handful of books, unlike Marlow. There was of course the slim paperback by Conrad. And Caesar's *Gallic Wars*, in which he described watching the blue-bodied Britons on the shore of the Thames regarding *him*, the foreigner, the alien, just as Elgar was when travelling down the Amazon in old age. I'd brought whatever geological data I could find about the Thames, sea journals by Gandhi, and the recently published book set a few thousand miles away in Sri Lanka, an artistic and archival work involved with the mapping of another supposedly far-flung 'darkness'.

And all the time while I was staying on the boat, I thought back to Conrad and his friend Ford Madox Ford in 1899, landlocked on a farm in Postling, Kent, carefully editing those first and last paragraphs of *Heart of Darkness* which depict the Thames and London. It appears to be the same landscape, *almost* the same, but not quite. For London, depicted as a great town at the beginning, is by the end a black bank of clouds over the river leading into the heart of an immense darkness.

This manuscript they were working on, published a few months later in *Blackwood's Magazine*, was expected to be just a small novel by Joseph Conrad, about a river journey.

Alain Mabanckou

London's Heart of Darkness

Translated from the French
by Sarah Ardizzone

It is Friday 13 July 2012.

In many European countries, and even in America, Friday the thirteenth is a day with a curse hanging over it. But Friday the thirteenth is synonymous with neither bad lack nor misfortune in the imaginations of the people in the country from which I come, Congo-Brazzaville, neighbour to Congo-Kinshasa, Joseph Conrad's legendary 'heart of darkness'. And so, with nothing to fear, I shall begin my account of this day …

When I heard about this location high above the Queen Elizabeth Hall and it was suggested that I might like to spend some time living in it, I nearly laughed out loud. I also made a mental note that the English really are the grand masters of black humour! But I was wrong: imagine my surprise on finding myself inside this reproduction of the boat in which Joseph Conrad sailed on behalf of the Congo Free State – this being the name of the vast territory over which Leopold II, King of the Belgians, had decided to exert his authority, making it his private possession. That territory was called Zaïre during the dictatorship of Mobutu, and today we know it by the name of the Democratic Republic of Congo. Congo-Kinshasa and Congo-Brazzaville are separated by the Congo River, but the two cities rank amongst the closest capitals in the world …

I am in the very heart of London, and yet I feel as isolated as Robinson Crusoe on his island. I must control my excitement and mounting sense of curiosity in order to imagine, for a little while, that I am on the Congo River, the river of my country, one of the biggest in the world after the Amazon, with its history unrolling before my eyes. For how can I be in the *Roi des Belges*, even if this is London, without reflecting on what took place in Africa towards the end of the nineteenth century? The dealings and negotiations that resulted in the plotting of the borders of the Africa we recognize today ...

The shadow of Conrad stalks this room, and I feel as if I'm living with him. I am, of course, surrounded by books and, above all, by different versions of *Heart of Darkness*: a graphic novel adaptation by David Zane Mairowitz, illustrated by Catherine Anyango, catches my eye. Perhaps, at night, Conrad emerges from his pages to tell the forlorn visitor about the odyssey of his character Charles Marlow, the British merchant-navy officer appointed by Belgium, who undertook to navigate a river in my continent?

I have the finest view of the Thames from my little Conradian refuge.

On the river, a few vessels pass by filled with tourists who give me odd stares and occasionally point at me, probably wondering what on earth a big black man is doing level with the rooftops of this city. Perhaps they think a film is being shot up here and that I am a stuntman doubling for the lead actor in the crucial scene. Unless they're mistaking me for an untalented burglar, or even a worker repairing the roof ...

I go into the saloon.

There is a secret window to the left, next to the one with glass in it that lets in the light.

I open this secret window and land on a glossary of nautical terms along with several representations of the Congo River, one of which is a view of the river taken from an aeroplane. The Congo resembles a long, lazy boa constrictor, replete but no longer sure in which direction to travel.

Behind the hidden window there is a second window, like a Russian doll. I open it and discover a black and white image of an old man with the long white beard of a poet in exile; like Victor Hugo, when, driven out by Napoleon, he sought refuge in Guernsey to write his pamphleteering volume of poetry, *Les Châtiments*.

Except that this man is not Victor Hugo. Beneath the photo I read the label: '*Roi des Belges*'. It is Leopold II, King of the Belgians, who was obsessed with creating a state in the Congo Basin and who relied on the services of the British explorer Henry Morton Stanley, with whom the king struck a deal in 1878. Stanley was similar to the character of Charles Marlow in Conrad's novel, and proof that Conrad was largely inspired by his accounts when he wrote *Heart of Darkness*.

How can we ignore the way the partnership between Leopold II and Stanley heralded the division of Africa? Indeed, Stanley would go on to purchase several tracts of land in the Congo for the King of the Belgians. That land became the king's private property and later on, in honour of the monarch, Stanley would even give the name of Léopoldville to a village, which has now become the capital of Congo-Kinshasa.

If the Belgians used a British man to 'grab' some of the lands on one of the banks of the Congo, on the other bank the French used an explorer of Italian origin, Pierre Savorgnan de Brazza, the man who opened up colonization in central Africa for France.

These, then, were the two great powers of the time (Belgium and France), which, in order to extend their influence beyond their territories, required the services of explorers from other powerful nations, Italy and Great Britain.

Belgium and France squabbled amongst themselves for the lands of the Congo, each nation claiming ownership. It took a Conference of Nations, the famous Berlin Conference in 1884, to assuage their appetites. Europe had come together in order to divide up Africa, thereby rubber-stamping the colonization of the continent. Belgium took possession of what is now Congo-Kinshasa, and France of Congo-Brazzaville, a territory that is small but rich in oil ...

I lie down in the bedroom. The copy of *Heart of Darkness* I am holding is a French translation, because I find it hard to understand all the English nautical terms used by the author. Conrad isn't far, I can sense him watching me turn the pages.

I close the book and my thoughts shift to all the criticism levelled against him – notably, some virulent criticism from Chinua Achebe. The Nigerian writer denounces the racism he detects in Conrad, who evokes a dark Africa where all that can be glimpsed is witchcraft and opaque protagonists who do not drive the book. They are merely 'material', the collateral of the author turning his eye on our continent. What matters for Conrad is the long journey, the ascent of the Congo River by his lead character, who is working for the Belgians. And so there is no internal gaze that might provide the reader with a sense of the soul of these people. But can we reproach Conrad now for his attitude, when in reality it was simply a reflection of what Europe thought of Africa at the time: a lost continent in which barbarism was the chief characteristic? Didn't this kind of thinking give rise to what was then called 'colonial literature', in which Europe explained Africa to the world in narratives from which Africans themselves were absent? Conrad, therefore, didn't hold back from using terms propagated in colonial literature that were often contemptuous, including calling Africans 'brutes'.

But we shouldn't blindly condemn the author: he, like his colleagues at the time, was only using Africa as a backdrop in an era when Europeans were thirsty for exoticism, for far-flung voyages to spice up the harshness of their cold climate. What needs acknowledging in Conrad is his caustic view of the abuses of his own civilization, of Western civilization. Conrad points his finger at colonialism and its excesses, particularly when he rails against the French bombardment of Dahomey.

Later on, other European writers would adopt the same spirit of denunciation. I am thinking of the French writer André Gide and his journal *Voyage au Congo*, published in 1927. Gide also sailed up the Congo River, but he made a point of recording the deplorable conditions in which the colonized peoples lived, and he held the concessionary Western companies to account. These companies maltreated the native populations by subjecting them to forced labour, and such maltreatment was covered up by the colonial administration. Despite Gide's journal appearing to be an inquiry into these abuses, the French author didn't question the colonial system itself! He even believed the authority of the white man to be necessary if the poor negroes were to avoid a fatal kind of chaos. So people were surprised, in 1928, when a politically engaged French writer, Albert Londres, published *Terre d'ébène*

(*Land of Ebony*), a journal of his experiences in West Africa, in which he clearly railed against colonization and accused it of perpetuating a system of slavery in which the Africans were victims, above all at the time of the building of the railways. Naturally, this book was bitterly criticized by a Europe whose expansion depended upon colonization thriving ...

It is late.

My eyelids are heavy with sleep, but I'm feeling peckish. I get up and head over to the kitchen, from where I can see the big wheel: a sort of giant fairground ride referred to by the English as the London Eye. At this hour, no tourist would be admitted into one of its air-conditioned cabins. Now one of the city's star attractions, it was built to celebrate the year 2000, hence its other name, the 'Millennium Wheel'. I imagine myself inside it, turning with history, but in the opposite direction, travelling back to the period when Conrad was inside the *Roi des Belges*.

What is the connection between this wheel and the boat taken by Conrad? I have no answer to that. Perhaps I have thought too much about the Congo, about colonization and the voyage along the Congo River? Consequently, anything that moves seems to me to be from another time. Life is a wheel that turns and may stop at any moment, I reflect as I return to my bed, with what's left of a sandwich in my hand.

I am going to sleep leaving the windows of this room open. When the first glimmers of dawn light up the sky, I shall feel as if the boat I am in is about to berth somewhere in Africa and that I shall be disembarking to meet new populations. I shall ask them whether they've heard of a boat called the *Roi des Belges*, and whether they once caught sight of the beard of a man named Joseph Conrad who bequeathed to posterity a masterpiece entitled *Heart of Darkness* ...

JULY

Geoff Dyer

Some Stories, with Annotations

Like *Death in Venice* or *The Great Gatsby*, *Heart of Darkness* is not just a book but a modern myth – everyone has read it, even if they have not done so personally. The actual book is far stranger than accounts of it sometimes suggest. It's a shame in a way that the book has become so famous as to dull our sense of this pervasive strangeness. Re-reading it now I find it scarcely less bizarre than when I plodded through it as a mystified seventeen-year-old. What H. G. Wells wrote of Conrad's earlier book, *An Outcast of the Islands*, also holds good for *Heart of Darkness*: 'his story is not so much told as seen intermittently through a haze of sentences'.

Strictly speaking, the book is narrated not by Marlow but by someone listening to him, someone who, exactly as prescribed by Walter Benjamin in the famous essay 'The Storyteller', begins his story 'with a presentation of the circumstances in which [he has] learned what is to follow'. (Had Benjamin read *Heart of Darkness*? The novel seems to affirm and then refute the essay's claim that the art of the storyteller has been undermined by … the novel!) This un-named listener – the reader's embedded representative – reports what has been said by Marlow, so that we peer at the narrative river through a forest overgrown with quotation marks. Much of the time Marlow seems simply to be waffling on – even more extraordinary given what a short book it is, how little room there is for waffling.

★

We are perched up on a roof high above the river but the weather has been so terrible, for so long, that the boat feels like a submarine. The over-boat has become a U-boat, at risk of flooding courtesy of what's above (rain), rather than the river below. My God – or by Jove, as Marlow likes to say – it seems like it could just float off the roof and slide into the river like a ship being launched up in Tyneside or Glasgow, where they don't make boats any more and where the weather has probably been – inconceivable though this seems – even worse than here.

I'll say this for the Thames though, at least it's not always bursting its banks – unlike some rivers I could mention, or would if I could remember their names. That one in Tewkesbury? Or Hebden?

I always love it, in films, when a submarine breaks the surface of the water and the conning-tower hatch is opened. It's not just the relief – the whoosh of sea air flooding through the cramped, feet-and-fart reek of the sardine corridor of *das Boot*; it's the fact of something coming into view, breaking through the barrier – yes, the *film* – separating the unseen from the seen.

It really feels like being on a sub when, with some difficulty – because of the Battle-of-the-Atlantic gale and the rain pressing down on it – I open the top circular hatch and slither out to take a look. We've broken the surface in the midst of the merchant (banking) convoy. It is – to shift terrain dramatically – a bit like climbing Everest in that no sooner have you got to the top than it's time to go down again. Jeez, it's like the Death Zone up there. And it isn't just the rain and wind and typhoon that made it so difficult to open the hatch: the sky is like lead, like lead I tell you, pressing down like the implacable burden of adjectival insistence.

A-levels: the start of reading literary criticism – and how boring that seemed, what a comedown from the novels themselves. For Conrad we had to read *The Great Tradition* by F. R. Leavis, whose analysis of *Heart of Darkness* was one of the first pieces of lit crit that I actually understood and learned from. It was still boring to read but I could see the point. Last year the art historian T. J. Clark told a story about Leavis, who, if I remember rightly, may have taught him at Cambridge. Leavis, Clark said, was driven mad by the institution, by Cambridge: a Kurtzian figure in the backs of beyond, amid the much-punted Cam and the brooding flatness of the Fens.

Conrad has generated an impressive critical literature. Readings of *Heart of Darkness* necessarily consider not just the book itself but previous readings. The result is a kind of critical river. Conrad is also, of course, the source of a creative river – a source which, in turn, has its own origins further upstream, further back in time (as Marlow describes his journey). To what extent does the creative river double as a critical river – and mirror?

*

CONRAD AND CÉLINE:

From *Journey to the End of the Night* (1932):

> 'Out where the Company's sending you, it's deep in the bush. Very damp! … Ten days' trip from here … First by sea … Then up the river […] the man

you're replacing at the post up there is a rotter ... just between you and me ... He simply won't send us his accounts ... Nothing we can do ... we've sent him letter after letter ... A man doesn't stay honest long when he's alone! ... You'll see. He's written, says he's sick ... Big deal! I'm sick too!'

And

I tried here and there to get a little more information, a few facts to go by. Because what the director had told me about Bikomimbo seemed incredible. Apparently the place was an experimental trading post, an attempt to penetrate the bush, at least ten days' journey from the coast, isolated in the midst of the natives and their jungle, which had been described to me as an enormous reservation, crawling with animals and diseases.

⋆

Pacing around is usually part of the choreography of anxiety but it can also be an indicator of pleasure: you don't want to be anywhere else but are too excited and full of anticipation to sit down. So, just in case you're on Waterloo Bridge and see a thin figure pacing around the boat house, rest assured – he's not in any kind of anguish, he's quite happy where he is.

⋆

CONRAD AND FITZGERALD (MARLOW AND CARRAWAY):

Fitzgerald was a far more diligent reader, absorber and learner than is often assumed. He aspired to 'do the wide sultry heavens of Conrad', he admired *Nostromo* (one of the most boring novels in the language) and hoped, in *Tender is the Night*, to achieve the 'lingering after-effects' that he associated with Conrad. Is Conrad there in *The Great Gatsby*; that is to say, is Marlow's voice there in Carraway's?

'Gatsby turned out all right in the end.' I hear a kind of negative echo of Marlow in this. Negative in the sense of positive, turned on its head.

> We were wanderers on a prehistoric earth, on an earth
> that wore the aspect of an unknown planet. We could
> have fancied ourselves the first of men taking posses-
> sion of an accursed inheritance, to be subdued at the
> cost of profound anguish and of excessive toil.

That's Marlow (whose journey takes him into 'a towering multitude of trees'). And this is Carraway (whose lawn, after a rain storm, is full of 'swamps and prehistoric marshes'):

> ... gradually I became aware of the old island here
> that flowered once for Dutch sailors' eyes – a fresh,
> green breast of the new world. Its vanished trees, the
> trees that had made way for Gatsby's house, had once
> pandered in whispers to the last and greatest of all
> human dreams; for a transitory enchanted moment
> man must have held his breath in the presence of this

continent, compelled into an aesthetic contemplation
he neither understood nor desired, face to face for the
last time in history with something commensurate to
his capacity for wonder.

★

Staying in a room that is not your own in your home city:
the fact that it feels so odd is a sign of how settled my life has
become. In my younger and more vulnerable years I often used
to wake up in other people's flats, either because I'd missed the
last tube and didn't want to fork out for a taxi or, less often,
because a romance had got underway. It's great being on the
boat but whereas, in another city, I would be impatient to get
out and experience the streets, the cafés, the shops, here I am
gripped by exactly the opposite sensation: that every minute
spent outside the boat is time wasted. Also the slight fear that if
I walked around the South Bank I might bump into someone
I know. Why *fear*? Because this feels illicit, as if – even though
I'm here on my own, waiting for my wife, as it happens –
I'm having an affair (for which this is the perfect venue). Also,
because it's my town out there, I'm conscious of the possibility
that the person I bump into might be myself.

★

CONRAD AND BORGES:

Last two lines of Borges's poem, 'Manuscript Found in a Book
of Joseph Conrad':

The world is a few vague tepid observations.

The river is the original river. The man, the first man.

★

Back in the days when the motor car was seen as panacea rather than intractable problem, did no one consider concreting over the Thames, turning it into a curving, twelve-lane freeway – with bridges over or tunnels under?

★

CONRAD AND DAVID LODGE:

The fun moment in *The British Museum is Falling Down* when a bunch of Chinese students is convinced that the desk Adam Appleby is working at in the British Library is the very one where Marx spent many years researching *Das Kapital*. Adam's response: 'Mr Marx, he dead.'

★

It's only five o'clock but already 'beastly, beastly dark'. The worst summer in living memory has generated a kind of contentment. None of the torment that usually goes with summer: will the weather be nice on the special weekend of … the wedding? the festival for which we bought tickets ages ago? the picnic with friends? A few more summers like this and the word 'picnic' will not just atrophy from lack of use, it will disappear from the language. People will have to consult dictionaries to look up its meaning when they come across it in novels: '(picnic, lightning)'.

★

CONRAD AND KAPUŚCIŃSKI:

A couple of years ago, right beneath where we are staying, I chaired a celebration of the life and work of Ryszard Kapuściński with Jonathan Miller and Michela Wrong (*In the Footsteps of Mr Kurtz*). A masterclass in failed chairing, the event took on a crazed momentum of its own and became a Kapuściński-dissing session. Elaborating on the argument advanced by John Ryle in a review of *The Shadow of the Sun*, Wrong insisted, essentially, that Kapuściński's methods were unreliable and unsound. All of which is a prelude to mentioning a surprising lacuna in Kapuściński's translated writings: no mention, that I can recall, of Conrad, whose name only crops up once in Artur Domosławski's new biography of Kapuściński. How strange that Kapuściński did not write more about Conrad as guide and inspiration, in the way that he wrote about Herodotus. It is almost – to use the Marlovian term – inconceivable that Conrad did not play a part in persuading him to lead the life of adventure and literature that he did.

★

Our epic non-summer has ended up being as stress-free as a season in Tuscany. We are resigned. We don't have to fret over whether to take umbrellas: madness to leave home without an umbrella and a rain coat. For the first time ever in England I have seen people *cycling* with umbrellas. If Darwin's theory of evolution is correct then umbrellas will eventually start growing out of people's heads, like antlers from deer. We live in July as if in November with extra hours of daylight (so-called) thrown in. One half of wisdom is not fretting

about what you can't change, so it's good to have made peace
with the weather. The feeling of contentment merges into an
inkling that one wouldn't mind no longer being alive, that it
would be a relief – to put it mildly – not to have to endure
such meteorological punishment. Because this 'contentment'
is only an inch from suicide, from chucking oneself in the
Thames. It's also a resignation that could erupt into its opposite, into a scream: not in Munchian reds and purples, just a
dreary charcoal smear of grey from the brolly tide of Waterloo Bridge – and not a scream at all, more like a whisper, a cry
that is no more than a breath.

★

CONRAD AND COPPOLA:

The genius *idea* of *Apocalypse Now*: a relocation of *Heart of
Darkness* to the Vietnam war, changing the Congo for the
Mekong, and casting Brando, the great method actor, as Kurtz
(even if that ended up being the worst thing about the film).
Coppola's wife made a documentary about the making of the
film. A director's cut of the film was later released. What one
longs to see, however, is footage of Harvey Keitel as Willard
before he was sacked and replaced by Martin Sheen. The
mythology swirling around this lost performance somehow
creates the illusion that it is Keitel, not Brando, whose method
was unsound.

★

We are as forgiving of the weather as fans of a consistently
losing football team: month after month of rain, wind and cloud

followed by a few afternoons of sun and we're not only happy but full of optimism, confident that things might improve, that – in football terms – we might stay up. By late August we will be mired, as usual, in a relegation battle, pinning our hopes on an 'Indian summer', resigned to going down but already – in spite of the evidence of years – looking for speedy promotion back to the premiership of sun next June. A recipe for despair.

*

CONRAD AND AMIS (TIMES TWO):

Martin Amis somewhere offers an excellent piece of advice on the limits of description. If something is 'indescribable', he says, then you're better off not describing it. A devastating critique of Conrad's method in *Heart of Darkness* – unless, as Walter Benjamin puts it in 'The Storyteller', what is being described is the way that 'the communicability of experience is decreasing'.

Maybe Conrad is there, glaring in on Keith Talent like the low and blinding sun at the end of *London Fields*: the 'Horrorday' with its 'horror clock', 'horrorteeth', 'horrorzip', 'horrorleaves', 'horrorshard' and so on.

*

All very well looking out of the window, seeing the green lasers come on beneath the bridge at midnight, but the cumulative effect of the familiarity of the outside world (London) and bad weather is … a frustrated urge to watch telly.

*

CONRAD AND DYLAN:

Allen Ginsberg in the liner notes to *Desire*: 'D. says he's reading Conrad storyteller, so hear continuous succession of Panama Hat Necktie details, exploding boilers and characters disappearing in tornados.' Except it turns out that, at the end of the song ('Black Diamond Bay'), Dylan is just watching a news story on TV – which he turns off and goes to get another beer.

★

The frustration of staying somewhere nice for just one night: always an incomplete experience, a twenty-hour day: 3 p.m. (check-in) till 11 a.m. (check-out).

The moment I check out I am my normal self again, one of the people I had been watching, hurrying across a bridge in the rain that has somehow turned to sun.

AUGUST

Teju Cole
Natives on the Boat

Two years ago, I was invited to a dinner party in New York. It took place on the Upper East Side of Manhattan, in a penthouse apartment. Our host was not merely rich: she had a name that through long association with money had itself become a shorthand for wealth. The dinner was being held in honour of a writer, by now old and famous, on the publication of his latest and perhaps final book. And because the book was about Africa, and because as a man ages his thoughts circle around questions of legacy, the writer, who was not himself African, had requested, in lieu of a normal book launch, a quiet dinner with a group of young African writers. This was how I came to be invited.

I stood in the luxurious living room of the penthouse, glass in hand, surrounded by Morandi's paintings and Picasso's prints. To the sound of a small bell, from a private elevator the old writer and his middle-aged wife emerged. He was short and stout – a little fat, even, though you could see he hadn't always been so – and he walked across the marble floor unsteadily, with the aid of a walking stick, and with the aid of his wife, a dark-haired, dark-eyed woman, taller than him, glamorous in her pashmina. My agent, who was also the old writer's agent, introduced us. 'Teju, meet Vidia Naipaul.'

The faint hiss of champagne being poured. The clink of glasses. Far below us was the muttering obscurity of the East River and beyond it, the borough of Queens, glimmering in the dark. In all that darkness was an infinity of information, invisible under the cloak of night. Vidia – please call me Vidia, he had said – whom the agent had told about my work on Lagos and New York, said, 'Have you written about Tutuola?' I said, no, I hadn't. 'It would be interesting,' he said. I demurred, and said I found the work odd, minor. There was something in Tutuola's ghosts and forests and unidiomatic English that confirmed the prejudices of a European audience. 'That's what would be interesting about it,' he said. 'A reconsideration. You would be able to say something about it, something of value.'

'There's a marvellous view from the roof,' our host said. 'Vidia's afraid of heights. He gets vertigo,' said Nadira, Lady Naipaul. And when the women had moved away, because I was nervous, because I wanted to show off a little for the master, I said: 'Maybe we don't all need the thrill of physical heights. Frank O'Connor writes somewhere that reading is another form of height, and a more perilous one.' 'Oh?' Vidia said. 'That's very good.' And we were called in to dinner.

I write these words in London. August has ended. I am sitting on the enclosed upper deck of a kind of boat. The sky is crisp and white, the sky which has returned to page one as it does each morning. Below, the busy little people begin to go about their day, inscrutable to the one who watches and unknown to themselves. London, from this peculiar vantage point, is precise as a print. Toy red buses cross and recross Waterloo Bridge as though maddened into repetition. St Paul's Cathedral leads white, the buildings across the skyline follow, white on white. The stone of London is white and pale, the sky is white and pale and beginning to intimate blue. Laden barges bring news

of the world in the form of goods. Above all this I sit on a boat
stranded in time's river.

At dinner, in addition to Sir Vidia and Lady Naipaul, there
was a well-known American actor, and his third wife. There
were Vidia's editor, our agent and his wife, our host, and three
other young African writers. The host's family claret was served
with dinner, served after a proud announcement of its prov-
enance, and poured almost ritualistically. Such things are bound
to disappoint, but this one was possibly the best wine I had
ever tasted. And, buoyed by it, we began to toast V. S. Naipaul,
who sat in his chair, bunched up in it, serene but a little tired,
nodding repeatedly, saying, 'Thank you, thank you,' with his
characteristic *bis*, the repetition of language that was second
nature to him. When three or four others had spoken, I gathered up my courage and said: 'Vidia, I would like to join the
others in celebrating your work' – though, in truth, the new
book, called *The Masque of Africa*, ostensibly a study of African
religion, was oddly narrow and stilted, not as good as his other
voyages of inquiry, though still full of beautiful observation
and language; but there is a time for literary criticism, and
a time for toasts. I went on: 'Your work which has meant so
much to an entire generation of post-colonial writers. I don't
agree with all your views, and in fact there are many of them
I strongly disagree with – ' I said 'strongly' with what I hoped
was a menacing tone – 'but from you I have learned how to
be productively disagreeable in my own views. I and others
have learned, from you, that it is fine to be independent, that
it is fine to go your own way and go against the crowd. You
went your own way no matter what it cost you. Thank you for
that.' I raised my glass, and everyone else raised theirs. A silence

fell and Vidia looked sober, almost chastened. But it was a soft look. 'Thank you,' he said. 'I'm very moved. I'm very moved.'

This vantage point above above the Thames – the sky is blue now, the 180-degree view of it full of long stratus clouds – in which the city is exposed to me but I am not to it, is a homage to Conrad's bitter vision. What might it mean when the native pilots the ship? What happens when the natives on the shore, numerous, unindividuated, are white?

Heart of Darkness was written when rapacious extraction of African resources by European adventure was gospel truth – as it still is. The book helped create the questions that occupy us till this day. What does it mean to write about others? Who are these others? More pressingly, who are the articulate 'we'? In *Heart of Darkness*, the natives – the niggers, as they are called in the book, the word falling each time like a lance – speak only twice, once to express enthusiasm for cannibalism, then, later, to bring the inarticulate report, 'Mistah Kurtz – he dead.' Otherwise, these niggers, these savages, are little more than shadows and violence, either in dumb service on the boat, or in dumb, grieved, uncomprehending and deadly attacks on it from the shore. Not only is this primitive, sub-human Africa incoherent to any African, it is incoherent to any right-thinking non-African too. A hundred years ago, it was taken as the commonplace truth. But we have all moved on. Those things are in the past, are they not?

'For the first four days it rained.' Vidia's face crinkled with pleasure. 'You like that?' 'I do, very much. It's simple. It's prom-ising.' 'I like it too!' he said. What I had just quoted was the first line of *The Enigma of Arrival*, his intricate novel about life in rural England. I value Naipaul for his travel narratives, for his visits to the so-called dark places of the earth, the patient way he teases out complicated non-fictional stories from his various interlocutors in Iran, Indonesia, India, and elsewhere. I like *A Million Mutinies Now*, *Among the Believers*, and the long essay 'The Crocodiles of Yamoussoukro', which, uncomfortable as they are in parts, also have the force of revelation. They are courageous not because they voice unpopular, and sometimes wrong-headed, opinion, but for the opposite reason: the books contain little opinion and are, rather, artful compressions of dozens of conversations. These are texts in which the natives, whoever they might be, speak for themselves – the difference with Conrad is glaring – and give an account, sometimes inadvertently, of their contradictory beliefs and ways of life, but also of their deep humanity. But it was *The Enigma of Arrival*, tirelessly intense, its intelligence fastened to the world of humans and of nature, that most influenced my own work, my own ear. I adore, still, its language, its inner music. In no small part, Vidia's writing held my interest because he, too, after all, was one of the natives. He too was thought savage and, in his cruel term, half-made. He was a contradiction like no other.

Dinner was over. We were in conversation, Vidia, our host, and me. He was in a good mood, flattered by the attention. Our host brought some rare books from her collection to show us. They were special editions of Mark Twain's works, and on the flyleaf of each was an epigram written by Twain and, below each, his signature. The epigrams were typical Twain: ironic, dark. And so we leaned over the old volumes, and Vidia and I squinted and tried to make out the words from Twain's elegant but occasionally illegible hand. We were sitting side by side, and Vidia, unsteady, had placed a hand on my knee

for support, unselfconsciously. I read: 'By trying, we can easily
learn to endure adversity. Another man's, I mean.' Laughter.
'To succeed in other trades, capacity must be shown; in the
law, concealment of it will do.' More laughter. Vidia began,
'You know, these remind me very much of ...' Ever the eager
student, I blurted out, 'La Rochefoucauld.' 'Yes!' he said, 'Yes!
La Rochefoucauld.' And with wonder in his eyes, the weight
from his hand and arm bearing down on me, he turned his
head up to our host, who stood just behind, and said, 'He's very
good. He's speaks so well, he speaks well.' And, turning back to
me, 'You speak very well.' In any other context, it would have
felt like faint praise. But we'd drunk claret, we were laughing
along to long-dead Twain, and I had managed to surprise the
wily old master.

Our host drifted away, and Vidia and I continued chatting
about this and that. Swift judgements came down. The simplic-
ity in Hemingway was 'bogus' and nothing, Vidia said, like his.
Things Fall Apart was a fine book, but Achebe's refusal to write
about his decades in America was disappointing. *Heart of Darkness* was good, but structurally a failure. I asked him about the
biography by Patrick French, *The World is What it Is*, which he
had authorized. He stiffened. That book, which was extraordi-
narily well-written, was also shocking in the extent to which
it revealed a nasty, petty and insecure man. 'One gives away so
much in trust,' Vidia said. 'One expects a certain discretion.
It's painful, it's painful. But that's quite all right. Others will be
written. The record will be corrected.' He sounded like a boy
being brave after gashing his thumb.

The party was ending. I said: 'This was not what I expected.'
'Oh?' he said, some new mischief in his eyes. 'And what did you

expect?' 'I don't know. Not this. I thought you'd be surly, and that I'd be rude.' He was pleased. 'Very good, very good. So you must write about this. You must write it down, so that others know. That would be good for you, too.' The combination of ego, tenderness, and sly provocation was typical.

Finally, after about twenty minutes, Nadira came for her husband. The hand lifted itself from its resting place on my knee. This benevolent old rheumy-eyed soul: so fond of the word 'nigger', so aggressive in his lack of sympathy towards Africa, so brutal in his treatment of women. He knew nothing about all this now. He knew only that he needed help standing up, needed help walking across the grand marble-floored foyer towards the private elevator.

The city below. The city at night, the city during the day. At certain heights, you get vertigo, but you also see what you otherwise might not.

SEPTEMBER

Ahdaf Soueif
Waiting for the Flood

I

Behind my left shoulder the giant wheel of the London Eye, behind my right the Wedgewood pastel of St Paul's – turn left, turn right, and in the space between the panorama of London passes before me: the Palace of Westminster and Big Ben with the tower of the Abbey rising behind them, Whitehall, Charing Cross Station, the building I've always thought of as the *Daily Mail*, the Savoy, Somerset House, and on and on to St Paul's. Icon after icon, like toys laid out in the window of a souvenir shop.

I have lived in and out of London for over thirty years. And I have seen this view countless times before. Not from this exact same angle, but from the pavement below, or from the various terraces of the South Bank Centre, or from the bridges, or … well, today it's different. Today I'm sitting cross-legged on an enormous bed; phones, laptop, diary, books around me, mug of tea at my side. At home – temporarily – IN LONDON.

Today, my first day here, everything is in headlines.

In the failing light a seagull wheels past my window.

A boat hoots on the river – the note foggy even though the light is clear.

The aircraft in the sky are so much smaller, more frail, than the oddly static Eye pods.

I climb out on to the deck and I see pyramids: the wire

109

pyramids holding up Charing Cross Bridge reflected upside down on the face of the station. Below me there are parasols, people, the bookstalls in front of the NFT packing up, lights coming on.

Whenever I'm near the National Film Theatre my father's with me – I keep my membership for his sake, even though he's eighty-eight and unlikely to travel from Cairo to catch a movie. He first brought me here, there, down there, when I was five. This is where I started to love cinema. And over there, across the river, where the lights have just flickered on, is where he took me to listen to the bands in bright uniforms. Were they military? I don't remember. And I don't remember paying particular attention to the obelisk over there – we had bigger ones at home. And there, at that point which I can't quite see, just west of Embankment Station, is where so many of us met on that morning of 2003, my mother and me and Ismail Richard, my younger son, and Sheila and Brigid and Alan and the Bloomsbury crowd and the *Guardian* crowd, and we started on the march: the march against the Iraq war that was to change nothing and change so much.

I watch the scenery change to party-time. The National Theatre's a flaming pink and Aldwych peeps out in purple from behind the staid white of Somerset House.

Why is it possible to feel instantly at home on a boat in a way that's difficult in a hotel, impossible in a just-moved-into house? The transient self becomes one with the transient boat, perhaps? Yet this boat is far from transient; this boat is berthed, perched, here, on top of a concert hall, looking out on the city, waiting.

When I go to bed I don't pull down the blinds. Surrounded

by light I fall asleep to the pops and creaks and thumps that I've – in a few hours – come to know, and ignore.

In the night an alarm goes off three times. The first time I wonder if I should get out of bed. After the second I can't sleep. The third finds me reading the words of my predecessors, the other writers who've slept in this bed, stood on the deck, watched the flow of water and traffic, contemplated the river, the city.

2

They invoke, my predecessors, as you would expect, past writings, and parents, and issues of belonging to this city, this civilization. And Conrad, always Conrad, since the conceit is that this boat we've all lived on is his boat.

Did Conrad belong here or didn't he? He made his name in English. Yet he writes of a man dying, in the middle of his family, speaking sadly in a language no one could understand. Well, I'm no Conrad but I've always been puzzled when asked about belonging. How English do I feel, I'm asked. And the answer is, not at all. But I feel comfortable. It has seemed to me that the available labels are wrong – that what is being asked is the wrong question.

Was Conrad racist? For me, it was clear when I read him that he expressed racist attitudes. And it was also clear that he was a brilliant writer. And I was glad when I found that Edward Said had dealt with all that – as I thought – once and for all. What seems more pertinent, I sit and think, is to look at how those attitudes manifest themselves today. Marlow, in that famous paragraph, ruminates 'The conquest of the earth ... is not a pretty thing when you look into it too much. What redeems it is the idea only. An idea at the back of it ... and an unselfish belief in the idea — something you can set up, and bow down before, and offer a sacrifice to ...' The idea/idol he's set up has not gone away with the collapse of the old empires; call the idea 'development', call it 'capitalism' or the 'free market', call it even 'democracy' along Western lines — the idea is the same idea, generated in the West and pushed on the rest of the world for the rest of the world's own good. But the idea doesn't just murder people in Afghanistan and Iraq, it doesn't just try to appropriate the revolution in Egypt, it decimates the citizens of its own countries.

Jack London wrote a hundred years ago of the disposable underclass in this city — the underclass that agrees to its own periodic culling. Across the Atlantic, a few days ago, a man who would be America's next president said that 47 per cent of his co-citizens did not concern him. And in Egypt today, after police had killed two more men, the people of Meet Ghamr marched with banners proclaiming: 'The men you killed were workers' — in other words, we do not consent to the cull.

It's late.

Fairuz Karawya's voice flows around me: 'Have you tried waking alone, walking alone, though the streets are full of people?' To my right Waterloo and to my left Charing Cross. Bridges and terminals. And into and out of them people walk. In that alley by the station my first love brought me to a secret bar. At that point, by the obelisk, I set a scene in my first novel. The obelisk and the kitchen towel by this sink, right here, are both made in Egypt, and so is Fairuz Karawya's voice that fills my — for-the-moment my — boat.

I stand at the kitchen window. Above the Royal Festival Hall, rising out of it, tall and slender, is a bullet pointed at the sky. A ring ascends it, and hanging from the ring are chairs, far-flung, whirling. They fly and whirl and circle for a few minutes. You can see people's legs dangling, imagine their hands gripping the chains. Are they laughing? Screaming? Or just keeping a grip? A brief moment and the ring begins its downward slide. And next to it, dominating the view, the aerated wheel of the London Eye, held together by what looks like string, a giant circle punctuated by pods peopled with tiny little dolls. You cannot see it turn but focus on an individual pod, and each time you look it will be in a different place. Its motion is perpetual, imperceptible.

It's late.

My mother in her last year had clocks hung on the walls in her living-room and her bedroom. In the hall. She wanted time to be no more than a glance away. My aunt Awatef's husband in his last few months kept demanding to know what the time was. 'Awatef!' he'd yell from his room and bring her hurrying down the long corridor: 'Awatef! What's the time?' It drove her mad. 'What appointments do you have?' she'd eventually shout back. 'What is it you'll be late for?' Edward, Edward Said – at the end – insisted something had gone wrong with his watch. Tonight I have two massive clocks to consult: the *Daily Mail*'s in front of me, flanked by the Union Jack and the Stars and Stripes. Big Ben on my left. It doesn't need to fly a flag.

In Parliament they're discussing, again, how to make public spending cuts and avoid raising taxes.

The rain begins.

What flood is this boat waiting for?

3

At the kitchen counter I consider making tea. In the great, solid bulk of the Royal Festival Hall there's a cut-out rectangle of a window. I guess from the height and stance of the people in the foreground that they're sitting at a bar. Others move behind them. In that rectangular frame they seem to be theatrical, choreographed, performing. Then I realize that's the members' bar, where I had sat, back in the summer, looking at this boat. I had seemed normal to myself then. Then, the boat was the surreal spectacle, sitting like a giant brown flightless bird, incongruous on the grey concrete. I had looked to see if anyone was in there, in the window where I am now, looked to see what performance this person was putting on.

I stand as still as I can. If someone looks over from the members' bar maybe they'll think I'm unreal, a cut-out, a prop.

4

Rain.

Always when I try to contemplate the Thames I end up thinking about the Nile: a river that works by simply existing and plants life in a desert, a river on which a queen set sail with her musicians in a boat hung with silk to meet the man with whom she would take on Rome – and fail, and break wide a schism between South and North for evermore.

Here there's no music, no purple sails – only the raindrops clinging to the windowpanes and the gulls wheeling in the distance and it will never stop raining. It will always be grey. I will never get out of here. My face on the *Roi des Belges'* octagonal table. It would make perfect sense to die here, with the grey rain lashing at the windows, screening the grey river, the grey city. The sound of the rain beating down upon this boat – the only water this boat will ever know. Grey puddles on grey gravel, grey river, grey city. I shall die here.

5

We have a meeting of the board of the Palestine Festival of Literature, PalFest. I don't die because I remember we have this meeting and I have to prepare the papers and make lunch. After my friends have exclaimed over the view we celebrate that we took PalFest to Gaza for the first time this year. We resolve to hold the Festival next year in Jerusalem, in Gaza, Nablus, Ramallah, Hebron, Bethlehem and Nazareth – somehow.

During the meeting a phone call from Cairo: *al-Shorouk* newspaper is adopting a campaign to stop the displacement of the poor from the heart of the city. Can I write 3,000 words?

And just downstairs, ten days ago, in the Queen Elizabeth Hall, people from this country and many others gathered to talk about the Arab revolutions, about the need for change everywhere – and to rock to Eskenderella, to music from Tahrir.

And I remember, back in '56, our flat in Stockwell filled with friends, English friends, as well as Egyptian and Indian and Syrian and German. And I remember the anger and the laughter and the flags and the marches and my mother explaining that our English friends were angry because England had attacked Egypt.

Shall we rephrase those questions then, about belonging?

Kamila Shamsie

A Room, With a View, of One's Own

I

Not a yellow brick road but a yellow door leads you here. This yellow door leading to an unpromising corridor with a paint-splattered cement floor – and that's exactly right. Enough of childhood's stories linger for me to know that places of wonder more likely exist through rabbit holes, through wardrobes, through paint-splattered cement corridors than at the end of frescoed hallways where knowing angels watch from gilded ceilings. At the end of the corridor, a button with an upward pointed arrow. I press it, and the steel doors open.

I've been warned by the ones who came before about the lift (though some called it the 'elevator'). Two minutes five seconds from departure to destination – a journey stubbornly refusing to progress with the seamless imperceptibility of the next-door London Eye. Instead, the lift rattles and whirrs just to let me know I'm going somewhere, on the move, to make sure I know that where I end up will be far far from where I've been. This, too, is exactly right. I have a friend whose workplace used to be a two-minute walk from her house. And though she is a woman of environmental consciousness, each morning she would get into her car, drive in a great loop for ten minutes, and then park a short distance from home – even in the depths of a snowy upstate New York winter. I wanted to keep the two worlds separate, she told me once. That story makes more sense

to me now than ever, in the two minutes and five seconds I rise
not very high yet very far from the world I leave behind – the
Known World, the Inhabited-By-Many World. Arriving here,
in this place so far apart, just a few seconds after leaving the
familiar streets around the Southbank Centre would be insuf-
ficient, slightly deranging. A journey – a voyage – is needed to
arrive at the *Roi des Belges*.

Steel doors open on to a raised cement walkway on the roof
of the Queen Elizabeth Hall, leading to an improbable aerial
vessel high above the bridges and barges of London. 'One ship
is very much like another,' Conrad writes in the opening pages
of *Heart of Darkness*. And yes, this ship is from the outside very
much like Conrad's own *Roi des Belges*. But to me it is like no
other ship. I have known I will live here for months now. All
year I've stopped on the pathways across the Thames, on the
south and north bank of the river, or on the top deck of buses,
looking up, seeking out this future home of mine.

When finally I open the back door – the only door – to
the ship and enter this space that appears much larger from the
inside than the outside – like Mary Poppins' handbag or that
old wardrobe – the ghost of Conrad does not immediately
greet me. A few short miles away is the home I live in every
day, presently filled with my closest family; much loved as they
are, their arrival has made writing at home impossible, forcing
me into the British Library – a glorious place, but lacking that
thing I am so desirous of when I sit at my desk: a window to
look out of, a view of the world. Now here it is, here I am,
here she is: not the ghost of Conrad but the presiding spirit of
Virginia Woolf, here in A Room of One's Own.

2

The wind is howling on this cold, cold autumn night as I push aside a paperback *Heart of Darkness* and reach for *The Common Reader*, in which Virginia Woolf writes about Conrad's early novels: 'Complete and still, very chaste and very beautiful, they rise in the memory as, on these hot summer nights, in their slow and stately way first one star comes out and then another.' I see only the brightest stars above the Thames – the lights of central London reach to the sky, so it is never really dark here, and I can't forget the city. My companions on this ship are the writers who have been here before – Juan Gabriel Vásquez, Jeanette Winterson, Sven Lindqvist, Caryl Phillips, Maya Jasanoff, Michael Ondaatje, Alain Mabanckou, Teju Cole, Ahdaf Soueif; late at night I look out at the lights strung along the riverbank and listen to the podcasts of each one's 'London Address', hearing the seasons drift past in their voices as they speak of winter and summer, of the Jubilee and the Olympics. They speak, too, all of them, of writers. Conrad and Conrad and Conrad and Conrad and Eliot and Eliot and Jack London and Jack London. Samuel Selvon, Rabindranath Tagore, André Gide, Peter Ackroyd, Chinua Achebe, V. S. Naipaul, Edward Said, Ernest Hemingway, Mark Twain. The world in a boat, the world of writers, the world of men. When Jeanette Winterson mentions Carol Ann Duffy it is the only invocation of a woman who writes.

3

Conrad wrote of women in *Heart of Darkness* in a way that anyone would find hard to remember. His voyagers, his explorers, the 'great knight-errants of the sea', as he calls them, are all men. Marking their line in Britain, he starts with Francis Drake and continues on to John Franklin. He forgets Lady Franklin, the first woman to receive the Royal Geographical Society's Gold Medal in 1860. Who can blame Conrad for that? Lady Franklin's medal wasn't conferred on her for any voyage of discovery but 'for self-sacrificing perseverance in sending out expeditions to ascertain the fate of her husband'. (This fate, when finally ascertained, was none too pleasant: stranded, his crew took to cannibalism. It's unknown whether he was eater or eaten, or both.) In the more than one hundred and fifty years since, only eight women have received the Gold Medal – Mary Somerville in 1869; Gertrude Bell in 1918; Doreen Ingrams – or, as she is named in the citation, Mrs Harold Ingrams – who received the medal along with Mr Harold Ingrams in 1940; Freya Stark in 1942; Monica Kristensen in 1989; Anne Stine Instad in 1991; Diana Liverman in 2010; Sylvia Earle in 2011.

Is it strange – or not at all strange – that travel writing has traditionally been so strongly associated with women but exploration is seen as a man's game? On this ship going nowhere, as I write, I am aware of two women who grew up in purdah, and first left that world of seclusion behind in order to travel. The first, my great-grandmother, Inam Habibullah, voyaged from India to England in 1924 to visit her three sons in boarding-school, where they had been sent by their Anglophile father. In London, as she related in her account of her travels, written in Urdu, she saw the sights, read newspapers avidly, was particularly interested in court cases, and was appalled by a play at the Haymarket which depicted an Indian as a savage who had failed to imbibe the humanity at the heart of Englishness. When it came time to return to India her husband suggested she might consider staying out of purdah – she agreed, but only on the condition that she would spend her time in the unsecluded world in service of her nation and community. She went on to become a member of the all-India Muslim League, was elected to the 1937 Legislative Assembly and was one of the moving forces behind the founding of the women's wing of her political party.

Her daughter-in-law, my grandmother, Jahanara Habibullah, also left purdah in order to board a ship. In 1930, aged sixteen, she travelled with her sister and parents to Switzerland, where her sister received treatment for tuberculosis. The scandal of the girls discarding purdah was so great that her sister's engagement was broken off by the family of her fiancé. Like her future mother-in-law, my grandmother never returned to purdah after her travels to Europe, and England – though the greatest transformation that occurred in her life was decades later in Karachi when her memoirs were published. The night before she died at the age of eighty-six, a few days before her book was published, she telephoned her sister-in-law to say: 'All these years I was turned into a housewife and made useless. I should have been a writer.' It was no coincidence that she started writing soon after my grandfather died – that's when she became a woman with a room of her own.

There will be no Gold Medals for my grandmother and great-grandmother; no Conrad will name them in the list of knight-errants of the sea. But now the rain falls around my flying boat, Billy Holiday sings the blues, and I try to step into their lives and imagine the London visible outside my window as it might have been in 1924, or in 1930, when it was the very heart of the darkness that was empire – and I know the journeys they made were not mere travel but exploration and discovery.

4

It is late now. I have stayed awake to watch the clock hands of Big Ben move backwards as British Summer Time ends. As I wait, I read the logbook of the *Roi des Belges* – everyone who comes here writes something, leaves a mark. I turn the pages; I read these lines:

> Why is no one in the Savoy hotel rooms? Why are
> all the lights left on?
> The Shard has disappeared
> Sax player has been replaced by a jack-hammer
> Woken by strange bumping sound. Can't see
> anything from the window. It can only be one thing:
> ghost sharks
> Fruit Vendors,
> Evangelists,
> Coffee Cups (Half Full),
> Church Bells,
> Road Works,
> Helicopters,
> Elevators

The head of a cloth camel.

Inside of eyelids.

What flood are we waiting for?

Where does the time go?

The bus I used to get to work is crossing the bridge
– looks like a doomed vessel.

Woken by a Mad Wind. Disturbing Dreams. The Eye
seems to have stopped.

Some part of me is prepared by all this for the moment I look out of the window twenty-five minutes before BST ends and see that the hands of Big Ben have already moved backwards, unseen by me.

Who else is watching? I Only am Escaped to Tell Thee.

The moon is full, or nearly so. A clock face without hands. Impossible to know if time is moving backwards or forwards.

I write to a friend who is writing far away to tell her of the clock famed for its reliability which moves back before its time. She replies: Proves what you can do HIDDEN IN PLAIN VIEW.

5

Up here, I'm hidden in plain view. Below, a world not thinking to look up for a writer with binoculars in hand. It's necessary, I realize, to go down into that world, before the view (all those little people!) becomes a way of seeing. In the morning – my body and the clocks in two separate time zones – I descend in the lift on a voyage back to earth. Two minutes, five seconds. Less than five seconds in, I am riveted, disbelieving: where there should be the lift manufacturer's name, I read ALIMAK. As an adolescent my absorbed mind turned words upside down, reading them back to front. Ot Eb Ro Ton Ot Eb. I knew the first ten or twelve lines of 'To be or not to be' backwards. So I remember, in a glance, the word ALIMAK. It's my name presented to me in the form of my own mind's games. I think, this must happen with all the writers that come here. The manufacturer's name spells out UJET for Teju, LEAHCIM for Michael, FADHA for Ahdaf. Of course it does. This is, after all, a lift to a world of enchantment, a lift to a room in which Virginia Woolf might write *The Waves* and not be swept away by them.

NOVEMBER

Adonis

Solo in the River Thames Orchestra

Translated from the Arabic
by Khaled Mattawa

I

A room/boat

(It descends from a cloud that descends from an impossible
    altitude.)

My bed is teetering: a wind without wisdom.

Am I being swaddled by a poem, or am I being rocked by
    a story?

The Thames rolls, rolling roped to its myths.

What will I write? Or how should I read London in
A Room for London, in a boat teetering above a tower?

I do not love the shores.
It's the pathways that London's anguish had made that I love.

And I ask Hamlet:
In what light have you landed,
and which passages of love's book have settled into you?

Should I write love like you while reading water,
should I write water while reading love?

I do not love the shores.
I have fortified myself.

It is a narrow world, like a deep puncture in a scream that has
    no wisdom.

And I ask London: what does the East read in you?
And these cities, East and West, are they anything other than
    carts full of limbs?
        Women, homeless
        their panties are their homes.
        Men, ships that see nothing but their wreckage,
            that do not see what they see.

And I say to London, Like you I have tried to read the
    stranger in me.
    Haven't you too asked yourself:
    Is this existence nothing but improvisation?

I had read *The Secret Agent*:
'If I do not murder, I will be murdered.'
        A miserable choice, indeed.
Is murder the origin of existence then?
And what is between them becomes a partner in divinity?

> No,
there is no other who is my enemy.
The stranger is another blood within me, I said
to London.

> But I do

> want the sky to surge against me.
This is how I'll know that my enemy is soaring like me,
that I'll live as if I'm warring against myself.

2

My dream does not tell me to become reality.
My dream has always been a wound, a wave of defection
balking, denouncing, raging: a world whose beginning
is the chatter of an apple lusting after Adam's lips.

O dream, tell London that the clothes humankind wove
     are dyed
with the ashes of their bitterness.
They build a road and get lost in it,
follow a route and their feet lead them to another.

Is there a future for dust except that it be dust?
Why then, O dream, do you listen for what remains distant
     and that has no presence?
What moves you to spill the wind and store the sand in a jar?
Will you remain in a forsaken desert in utter gloom?
How then can I free another, when I myself am not free?

I continue to live and work, a picture in my hand,
a picture that lives and works in the hands of a doll.

3

And I ask London: are you a mother, or are you the father
      who will be killed?
I am not one who'd say, London is a mother. I say, departure
and roving in roads that have no destinations.   I am not like
others who visit her, who want to know everything,   with
their eyes and hands,   and boast, I've read her page by page.
I do not love the city blurred by the glow of its pearls,
I love the city as a sea of loss that can never be tracked, that
      has no access.

The winds continue to blow from their sources.
We do not see how they begin, how they become,
how they reach us.

I love the city woven in   its secrets
and I prefer that my time dissipates in the company of
      people, walking as if we are a river, each of us solitary
      and alone.

I am not among those who say London is a mother, and who
      sleep in her shade, raising her name as a banner.

Shakespeare was the first to say, 'No!' to her conventions. He
      built in her a London that belongs to him alone.
Beautiful, what he saw. And my voice here descends from his.

People's cities belong to love and poetry, to thought and art.
They thrive there, or they grow savage and rot in narrowness
    and wretchedness.

And I say, Improvise, O night,
play on,
          on your flute,
play as if you are the sun itself.

It is beautiful, thrilling, that London's chords are like her
    objects.
In every market the scents of nymphs and fairies,
          not the scents of paradise,
sexual shapes, restaurants,   business offices
worship offices,   lords of dice,   lords of butchery,
massacres of lawful meat,   books residing in his waste
land,   celebrating Eliot or condemning him,   amusement
parks,   temples for every art,   human rights protected
here   and trampled with impunity there,   a hell of
hypocrisy,   two-legged cars,   others with four, arrow
and bow,   a small black stone on the door of a white palace.
The asphalt of this alleyway is from the East and the cloud
that washed it comes from the West,   bread that God
hands out among his children,   a poor one on the left,
a prince one on the right.
It's the way the Just and All Mighty one divides.

Hey, Policeman! There's an old lady crossing the road. Help her!

Here's an Arab man raising a banner,   a policemen riding
    a horse.
Signs that say Nature is dead and industry has become air,
    water, and sun.
Signs that salute our descent on the summits of stars.
Is this Qais? Is it *Hamlet?*
It seems that a gentle madness is building gentle bridges
    between culture and nature.
No poetry, no science, without the nectar of madness flowing
    in its veins.

And I hear the bustle of an argument between blacks and
whites, blacks and blacks, whites and whites, and women here
and there:
    diaspora and silence.
Sometimes I see in the eyes a glimmer that blames the lips
    for their silence.
Sometimes I see on the lips signs of dissent, and I see many
    walk away, and many stay on.
My ink delights in inscribing what an earlier Arab poet had
    said:

> *I open my eyes when I open them*
> *finding many there, but finding none!*

4

Since Gilgamesh, roots have been travelling in us, toward
    what is nothing but loss and bewilderment.
Become a friend then, to Gilgamesh, to one who does not
    know what surrounds him,

who knows not what he was, or what exists, or who he is.
The mud of creation's myth has become   a free language.
They cut nature's throat and strove to uproot her arteries.
They have turned money into a god and a throne,

      a singular blood.

           Ruin is the prince of space
           in the name of sky.

Money longed for, even if it were death.
Wait. Are you afraid? (Shall I name you?)
But in darkness, like another darkness, you have to wait.
These pitch black skies have defeated us;
there is no conqueror but they.
There is no conqueror but God.
What am I saying!?
I am saying identity is fraught with its opposites.

5

The Thames,   its shores are drawn by oceans.
           Shores, sheets
           of paper among which I'm flying.
My life is not a platoon and my language is not an army.
I imagine Eliot reading this poem.
Eliot, I belong to no past   and if I dream of a day to return
it is not that I'll become free in it,   but be free from it.

The site of the earth   is a cemetery and dust,
the son feeds   on his father's rage.

The road that now rises from the Thames toward the oceans
      has no water in it.
                (Who will tell Eliot that his land is still
a waste?)

              And the horizon's face?
You'd grow confused if you yearned for it.

Will you call it a grave? An axe?

             (Who will tell Conrad
that the oceans now only know how to breathe dust?)

The air, all of it, a curtain   of blood
and iron.
           Who will ask the oceans: do you remember
those who released their secrets to your depths, and departed?
They dared, and told the shores their news. Myths chased
them and killed them, and threw their corpses
where the waves know not how to speak of them.

And the Thames runs in two orbits: the war of kings and
      banks,
the captains of wind and profit,
and the war of longing
                for the warrior's return.

The Thames is a conquest, a warehouse where loot is stored.

And the hunt for gold has not stopped, has not ended,
and the groaning of the cities, anger's fire, has yet to end.

Myth tyrannizes us,
the reptiles of our forests mock us.
We disintegrate,   the soil avoids us.   Its grasses and its
          herbs
abandon us.   A roving disease,   a sick roving.

Cats and dogs in the houses of progress, have died and
          continue to die,
and we must remain prepared to weep over the coffin of
          civilization.

Or celebrate bequeathing her children (her beautiful puppies
          and kittens),
our wheat silos, and our property,
and listen to her bawl, Oh my crown, Oh my ivory, Oh no!
          Oh no!

The earth is not earth under our feet.
Truth is like nature, a freedom that is free.

How else can I face this truth of our age?
We enter it, and leave it. We travel on
the ships of conquerors, tyrants, shepherds of plentiful
          flocks
          as if we do not see   a human face on them.

We see   creatures made of iron
and plaster,   some dead,   some moving
    about awaiting their death,
people who know only how to progress toward their torn
    limbs.
In nightmares – in no other place do they live –   each
    a prisoner to his nightmares.

I am not like you, stranger, who are like me   I have no
    right to descend into my blessed fire.

I am not like you: the history of my earth still shifts to and
    fro in the darkness of crime.

6

Why, Ulysses, did you go to that abyss of darkness?
What did you expect?
'One day, my winds led me to it, and it tore me.'

I watch my body before me, behind me, around me.
I touch its limbs and wrinkles.
And I ask myself, how was I able to remain other than a hue?
And what will remain of the world that has made us
    misplaced,
that we butcher ourselves for?

On the road to you, I saw love, bewildered, taking off its coat,
    absent-minded, lost,
sidewalks tossing his innards and days about.

And I looked at an owl
where night is sleepless in her head,
a wise owl smitten with a temple;
she never reveals the names of those who worship there.

And I saw foam in the hands, its bubbles whispering:
'Ulysses hid hardships and secrets in the ocean
        so it would become his companion and rival.'
And the bubbles whispered:
'The waves travelled in us, and told us that the clouds
are fruit that descends from the wombs of the stars,
and like a butterfly the sky used to fly to its cocoon.'

On the road to London I watched roses dance as they built
        beautiful huts to house their perfume.

I saw night walking barefoot toward his promise, singing:

        'I'll make a boat
        and when it cries "Port!!"
        the pathways will reply,
        You must learn to love
        to live on the galaxies' dust.
        Like a thread fallen
        from the buttonhole of space
        you must learn to remain.'

This is how I will fortify myself against these shores:
        with wind sometimes

and with light at other times
and with clouds as well.

This is how I will learn to not travel
except when the wind is a sail in my hands.

I love how water tells everything to everyone.
It bends to see things close to its chest,
carrying in its steps the inhale of its springs,
arguing with a flower,
and pleading
with a stone that prefers to speak in whispers.

Will anything remain
that allows for rebellion under the sun? (Listen, Ulysses!)
Or will the winds
of myth mock me?   My life a war, war in my life
as a child and an old man   and war   around it,
war between what was the beginning   and what will be
the end.

I do not need victory,   I do not fear defeat.
No witness.   No victor.   It is night: night
that embraces the world's body.
Night, an end just like the beginning. Night again.

7

I drink a river now?
From a stream of sparks flowing from the West,   I hear

'Do not be a sword handle,
be a free hand.'

And I ask Ulysses,
How do you write an ending and endlessness in one chord?

Ah Ulysses, my freedom
is no longer free.
My freedom has yet to free itself.

Colm Tóibín

Boats

'Life and death?' Williamson asked. 'Do you mean both?'

'Yes,' the old man replied quietly, moving his two fingers towards his lips. He inhaled, filling his lungs with satisfaction as though he were still a smoker. It was one of his habits. He thought for a moment.

'Yes, both.'

'And they believed they were the same thing?'

'No. Like all of us, they understood the difference perfectly. I mean, how could you not?'

'But then surely …?'

'Yes, I suppose it might seem odd. You know, I never discussed it with anyone during my two sojourns on the island and my other stay on the neighbouring one. It was somehow not open for discussion. Not much was open for discussion, which made time there very agreeable. That is, before the attack. I think the attack destroyed everything. Well, I am sure it did.'

Williamson had come to enjoy his wealth, or the wealth his wife possessed. He had married late and had, we knew, taken his time to adjust to his new domestic circumstances. His wife was a great talker. He liked to say that he bought the boat to get away from her chatter, but I believe, in fact, that she bought it for him because she needed time away from his silence.

It had been a perfect day's sailing and the crew of two had gone to get some spare part for the boat. They had left us alone in the dwindling light as the tide began to turn on the great river and we waited for Williamson's driver to come and collect us. We had tied up at Deptford at the usual place close to the small culvert, having come in an hour earlier than expected. All three of us watched the stillness in the water, as though the water's breath were being held. We stood looking as the boats around us slackened on their ropes and then slowly turned.

As usual, it was relaxed and easy between the three of us – between Williamson and myself, who had shared lodgings in Hong Kong after the war, and the old man who had sailed for many years in the South China Sea and had come home when air haulage had taken over many of the old trade routes, and when policing some of the ports in the East had become more efficient. Things were more relaxed between us, indeed, since the death of Henry Bacon, who had come with us on these excursions before his illness. H. Bacon, as he was known, usually enjoyed an argument and was sure to contradict any remark made once the humour took him. He had now taken his opinions, many of them tedious, to the grave.

We did not replace Bacon, and this meant there was an added peace between us which came from his absence. The lovely idea that we were, all three of us, too old now for novelty seemed to give us satisfaction.

The old man had roamed that part of the world uneasily. When he made money he did not, as others did, settle down, keep a wife and family in Kent or Sussex while he sailed out once more to support them. He spent what he made on disappearing; there was much talk about him, as he was often left ashore, alone and unarmed, on islands on which no Englishman had yet set foot, or islands on which no Englishman, or Dutchman indeed, had stayed for very long. And then he would be found six months later rounding up a crew to take some goods – tobacco often, but also I believe contraband – from one port to another. He knew the reefs and the remote islands, it was said, as no one else in those years, and it was agreed among those I knew, even as late as the fifties, that if anyone went in search of him, or if anyone sought to intercept him, they would not find him. He was perhaps the last of a kind.

'They believed in nothing except boats,' he went on. 'The sun or the night or the sea itself didn't seem to interest them. And they had no artefacts or icons, which was rather a relief. And they did not paint the boats, or decorate them. Wood, of course, was scarce and that made the boats important. They traded what they produced for planks, or dead trees. They produced fruit of course, too much of the bloody stuff, but the main thing they produced that could be traded was called *palimene*, which was a sort of berry. If you rubbed it thoroughly on meat or fish, or indeed a dead body, it would preserve it for months and maybe more. You did not need salt. It was unique to the island and in great demand by the other islands. It gave things a delicious flavour, it was like lemon but darker and richer. I always thought I could have made a fortune had I cleared the place of most of its inhabitants and cultivated the stuff. I think it was all destroyed with the fire so we won't have that to fall back on when the refrigerator fails us.'

He said the word 'refrigerator' with immense distaste, but it was the word 'fire' that I noticed, the casual way he said it.

'And the boats?' Williamson asked.

'What I understood was that they took the view that a boat, once made, had powers.'

He seemed to feel that he had said all he needed to say on the matter of boats. He stood up and stretched and then checked for a moment in the direction of the road as though he were impatient to get away.

'So they worshipped boats?' Williamson asked.

The old man did not reply. If he were lost in thought, then the thought seemed to be about some other matter. A sound came, like a car approaching, but it did not come closer and then it faded.

I found myself shivering. It was something about the silence, but it also had to do with the breaking of silence. We had all seen things or felt them. I had been interned by the Japanese in the war and I had marks to show for it. Williamson, too, had his wounds but they came from before, from his father, who was a great brute. But I knew about this only because of the nightmares he had in those years when we lodged together. He had never willingly spoken of them, as I had never spoken of being tortured, and never indeed been asked by these two men to explain the burn mark across my back and the opening in my stomach the size of a grapefruit, or the strange catch in my voice.

The old man was not a salty dog who told stories. Like us, he had met those types and found them worth avoiding. What made me shiver now was that I found his need to explain this business of the boats was unlikely, unworthy of him. It was all the more irritating because it came from a need that seemed to have been there all along, something merely suppressed or held in check until now. He was giving in to it and I disliked being in his garrulous presence while it happened. I had presumed until then that the friendship between us three and

H. Bacon was based most firmly on the idea that we disliked stories and story-tellers and tales of islands and the time before the war or the war itself. All of us, I understood, had much to be silent about.

As the clouds became darker, and a small wind seemed to blow up, I shivered again. I noticed Williamson watching me, uneasy too, or bored, or sad.

'They embalmed the dead and kept them close by and then, when the time came, and the tides were right,' the old man went on, 'they released them, sent them out by boat. To wherever. Not to return in any case. They seemed to have no problem about losing the boats. What was strange also was how at certain times the islanders kept away from their boats, left them on the beach. No one even went near the beaches then. And later, when the moon was almost full they would approach and pray. At least it sounded like prayer. If there were births, they happened in secret, but on these nights they were revealed. The women came with babies towards the boats and put them in one of them, and then they pushed that boat out with other boats to guide it and they did a circle of the island, all the time safely guiding the unmanned boat with the babies inside. It was done in silence.'

He stopped again. I wondered what this might have been like had H. Bacon been here, at what point he would have interrupted and stopped this. The sky was darkening now, and there was a band of flaming red over the city to the west. I felt free to study it as it faded and sank and gave way to a band of yellow light and then dark clouds, made all the darker by the edge of faded light around them.

'Sometimes, planks from the boats sent out would be washed

up,' the old man eventually continued, 'and that was how they knew that the dead had not found rest and there would be many days of further silence on the island. I do not know what resting place they had in mind for their dead, but I do know that not to arrive there was to live for ever in some dark state. No single body was ever washed up on the beaches, by the way; that would have been unthinkable somehow. Maybe the *palimene* caused bodies to sink in water.'

He spoke as though his story had just begun and would conclude far away from this version of island belief, or magic, or whatever it was. When I turned I found Williamson with his hands covering his face. It struck me then for a moment that there had been a story, a story I had heard years before, that implicated the old man in something. I had heard it in Macau from an Irishman who was drunk. I noted the name, the name of the old man, whom I knew at that time by sight and reputation. In those years there were always stories, especially about those who came and went and seemed to have knowledge of the inlets and the islands. Also, in those years, when my wife had left me, I drank and often craved company late at night. I heard more stories then than I cared to hear; I heard many of them twice or three times. But many of them too were only half told, as this one I heard from the Irishman about the old man was, but I remembered it, or most of it.

It made sense that someone who moved as the old man did in the years before the war had such stories told about him. It also seemed reasonable that the story, such as it was, might even be true.

'I knew the Englishman Fleming,' the old man went on. 'He made his money in arms, which was more dangerous than opium, and more lucrative. Once, only once, I had covered for him, and he was grateful for that but knew not to show his gratitude in any public way. He paid me, but knew not to greet me no matter where he met me. He now arrived on the island with two Malay servants. There were rumours about him and his taste in servants but that is another matter. They almost saved his life, the two of them, there is that to be said. But in doing so, of course, or failing to do so, they caused even more trouble than Fleming caused.

'I wish I could say that Fleming meant no harm. There was no evidence that he did mean harm, but I had never known this to be the case before, so I must presume that he had a plan, a reason to set up temporary house on the island, to have the two servants and a few others build him a dwelling from sand and bamboo. Perhaps, like me, he understood the value of *palimene* if it could be planted commercially. But I do not think he had a great interest in rare plants. Perhaps he was hiding from someone. He must have done quite a bit of hiding, especially in the years when he armed some Chinese rebels and some Muslim groups in Malaysia who needed to defend themselves. In any case, he slept on his boat with his rifle close to him and some loaded pistols while the building was going on.'

'I would have left had there been a way to leave. And it would have helped him, of course, had he spoken to me. When we met one day, he smiled in a way which was knowing and wicked and sly and then he passed on without speaking, followed by his two servants, who looked sullen when they caught sight of me. Since it was some months since I had seen someone from home I could have done with a few words with anyone at all, even Fleming, but I did not look back at him or his two servants. I imagine he did not look back either. One of them, by the way, was quite remarkable-looking. I mean striking.

'I could have told Fleming had he asked that he must not use the planks that were washed up on the beach for any purpose. And that he should keep away from the beach when there were boats there. But in those first weeks there were no boats on the beach. The ones the island owned had been used just before Fleming's arrival to ferry the dead away. The islanders watched for planks that might be washed up; they watched in case the sign came that some of their dead had not made it to their destination.

'And when some planks drifted in with the waves, they moved into their ritual of silence. Even the children knew to be silent, and the babies too, for all I know.'

'I found out the planks were missing from where they had lain on the beach the same morning it was noticed by the islanders. I wondered later if they came to me first to make sure that I did not have them. When they saw that I indeed was not in possession of them, they went to find Fleming. He was there, overseeing his new place of shelter. He was armed. He had his rifle and his pistols. And he had the planks. When they demanded he hand them over, he refused. When they insisted in very strong terms, he shot two of them. I heard the shots and I knew to stay where I was. I would have to make clear as best I could that this had nothing to do with me.

'Fleming and his two servants made it back to their boat after the shooting, by swimming, or so I understand. Fleming would not have been a great swimmer. He was a fat, ungainly man and I don't think he took naturally to water. By the time he and his two Malays were trying to get the engine started, a number of the islanders had swum underwater and were already under the boat. And they appeared on deck, indeed, before they had even been seen in the water. They wanted only Fleming and they took him off the boat in a great burst of yelping and calling on his part. They ducked him well in salt water as they dragged him back to the island. He was on shore again before he knew where he was. The servants, once they had the engine working, moved the boat away. No one tried to stop them, which in retrospect of course was a mistake. In fact, it was to prove the undoing of the whole island.

'They were rather proud of what they did with Fleming. They invited me to come and see it several times. It involved a breed of ants that they must have kept especially for such an eventuality and some sugary substance, almost hard like glue that they wound around Fleming, whom they stripped naked for this purpose. They tied his hands behind his back and left him sitting. They even fed him and gave him water over the days that followed as the ants slowly went for the sugar and then the skin and the organs and whatever else was there.

'Whatever pain Fleming felt at first was nothing to what came later. That must be said. The ants were tiny little things and they took their time. They seemed to have a sting, but not at first. I wondered if the sting was provoked by the sound of a man screaming. It was four or five days before the work was finished.

'By this time a small ship had appeared on the horizon accompanied by Fleming's boat. What was extraordinary was that the islanders seemed not to be worried about this. They had never been shot before, as far as I could make out, or had planks stolen. And they associated all this with Fleming and

Fleming alone, as though he were some sort of solitary demon wandering the earth, pink and fat and pleased with himself, and he had now been put paid to. So they let the boat and the small ship come close and they seemed pleased when a rowing boat was lowered from the ship and a number of armed men appeared. Two of them were Dutch and there were a few others I could not easily place. One of them spoke English and another seemed to be able to make himself understood in the islanders' language.

'The islanders took these newcomers to see what was left of Fleming as we might take visitors to the Lake District or the British Museum. A mixture of mild duty and pride of some sort, but more a feeling, it seems, that not to have shown the visitors Fleming's whitened bones might have deprived them of one of the sights. It did not occur to the islanders who did the showing, as far as I could make out, that the wider world did not share their own particular reverences. I imagine people take the same view of the Church of England or the Roman Church and suppose that these religions are known about worldwide and that the truth of their doctrines is somehow self-evident.'

'I imagine that too,' Williamson said drily.

It was now dark and I felt a cold coming from the water, the beginnings of a night-breeze. I could not see the old man but I could get a sense of Williamson close to me. I could hear his breathing and feel that he was listening with care now to what was being said. In all the years not one of us had ever spoken like this. We had confined our speech to comments on the wind and the tide, and perhaps the temperature. In all the years, too, Williamson's driver would have been here early and would have been waiting for us. And also, if the crew went somewhere they normally came back soon.

In all the years as well, H. Bacon would have interrupted any one of us who spoke at all, forced us to change the subject, or more usually forced us to say nothing more.

'When Fleming's supporters found me,' the old man continued, as though he had not been interrupted, 'they gave me a choice. I could stay on the island or leave it. If I left, it was agreed that they would drop me quietly on a neighbouring island some distance away and they would never say they had seen me. The idea that I would deny seeing them did not need to be mentioned.

'I knew they had some kind of retribution in mind, but I don't think they were sure what form it might best take. It helped their resolve, I think, that they were shown the ants by the islanders later that day. The ants were happy little fellows, replete after their feast, being held in case they were to be needed again. The ants helped steel their resolve, or so they told me. Once they managed to ascertain in full how Fleming had met his end, how long it had taken and how generally noisy it had been, they made up their minds.

'The islanders were rather anxious to share all the information about Fleming's demise. It was, after all, a matter of pride with them, and they seemed to feel that the visitors would share their pride, or be glad at least that it had happened. The visitors of course were careful to show no emotion one way or the other. They were armed and that might have helped. The islanders were not skilled at reading emotion. I think they thought the visitors were going to depart soon, having supped with them, or that they might stay a while longer and enjoy the large and abundant supply of fruit and maybe come to visit the two shot men, embalmed perfectly now by the *palimene*. The dead in many homes on the island were given the best, or at least the most prominent place, to sleep, and were propped up outside during the day as if to enjoy better the sunshine and the scenery.

'It is hard to remember at what point it was decided to burn the island,' the old man continued and then stopped.

In the silence that followed, I felt someone grip my upper arm and I knew it was Williamson. Williamson, who was always a great listener, must have, I imagined, heard the story too about the old man that I heard from the drunken Irishman in Macau. He had known, I surmised, the story of the fire before the old man came to it. I should have always presumed that he had known this story.

'What were you doing on the island?' I suddenly asked the old man.

'What do you mean?' he asked.

'I mean in the first place. What were you doing there? What were you doing on the island in the first place?'

'There were always reasons,' he said in a whisper. He made that simple sentence sound like a threat. But it was more than a threat. He had for a few seconds lost his ease, his composure, his contentment at being with friends on a boat after a good day. I reached over and touched Williamson's shoulder.

'What happened?' Williamson asked. And when the old man did not answer, he asked the question again.

'What happened?'

'They had made up their minds what to do,' the old man said firmly, coldly. 'They planned it carefully and deliberately and they moved fast. They had combustibles on board which they placed in the rowing boat and then got them on to the island. They knew what to do, what plan to follow. They knew to go right around the island and then start the fire so it would spread. It was easy once it began.

'By the time we were moving away, it was a conflagration. I expected to hear shouts, but I heard nothing. I expected to see figures running from the flames into the water, but no one appeared on the beach. You see, these people, they accepted death. I had not known that about them, or perhaps I had, but had not seen it put to the test. I suppose I knew very little about them in the end, whoever they were.

'After the war, when the British were making more accurate maps of those islands, they went there, the cartographers, and found nothing. You know, I was consulted as one of the few who had known the islands before the war. But of course I had no interest in going back. It was surprising, however, to be told that the cartographers and their helpers found nothing at all. No sign of anything. No *palimene* obviously. But nothing else either. No water table. No evidence that there had ever been fresh water on the island. It was abundant during my stay. I suppose they did not look carefully enough. And of course no boats or any trace of boats.'

'And that was that, then?' Williamson asked.

'Yes,' the old man said. 'Yes,' he repeated with even greater certainty. 'That was that.'

Williamson moved as the sound of a car came and the head-lights beamed across the mast of the boat. It was the crew. Soon a second car came, the sound of the engine like a soft purr. It was Williamson's. His driver beeped the horn once, as he usually did to let us know he was waiting.

As the other two made their way up the steps to the car, I stayed behind. I thought they could do without me for a few moments as I stood to look at the lights of London rising faintly over the west. I thought then of the outsides of the houses stretching from the city into the suburbs, the windows, some dark and some lit, the painted front doors. And inside, people preparing for the night, or having a meal, or talking, or reading, or listening to the radio or watching television. Some alone; some with others. My mind moved away from them, into the unoccupied rooms above them and around them, rooms with no lights on and doors closed or ajar, and within them the smaller spaces, the cupboards, the presses, the dressing-table drawers, all filled with things, but hidden away, not to be opened until something was needed.

I watched the lights flickering on the horizon beyond the river, and pictured those walking on the streets or sitting in cars. People like ghosts of themselves, silent, wary. Or people sitting opposite each other on the tube or the bus catching each other's eyes for a second and then glancing away. I wondered about the old man and the years I had known him. It was as though knowing him had been nothing more than a distraction. I wondered if he needed us to know him more, if that had been part of his plan, if he had come to the boat that day with such a plan in his mind or if it had all come of its own accord.

I stood and waited until his voice came from above, the voice severe, beckoning, in control, telling me that the car was waiting and we would have to go.

Acknowledgements

A Room for London was a major new collaboration in 2012 between Living Architecture and Artangel, in association with the Southbank Centre. A one-bedroom architectural installation in the form of a riverboat, it was designed by David Kohn Architects in collaboration with artist Fiona Banner.

The Artangel programme on board A Room for London was supported by the London 2012 Festival and Arts Council England. *A London Address*, a series of monthly writings and recordings, was commissioned by Artangel and presented in collaboration with the *Guardian*. The majority of the books in the Room's octagonal library were kindly provided by Foyles.

Artangel would especially like to thank Sarah Ardizzone, Claire Armitstead, the British Council, Iain Chambers, Rachel Holmes, Sophie Howarth, Khaled Mattawa, Tom Oldham and the Embassy of Sweden for their contribution to *A London Address*.

Λrtangel is generously supported by:

Supported using public funding by
**ARTS COUNCIL
ENGLAND**

ARTANGEL INTERNATIONAL
CIRCLE

Lauren Bon

Inge and Cees de Bruin

Andrea and Guy Dellal

Marie and Joe Donnelly

Tania and Fares Fares

Wendy Fisher

Mala Gaonkar and Oliver
 Haarmann

Samantha and John Hunt

Elizabeth Kabler

Jennifer McSweeney

Catherine and Franck Petitgas

Gilberto Pozzi

Pascale Revert and Peter
 Wheeler

Barrie and Emmanuel Roman

Cora and Kaveh Sheibani

Manuela and Iwan Wirth

Anita and Poju Zabludowicz

Michael Zilkha

SPECIAL ANGELS

Stephanie and Philippe Camu

Julie and Fred Chauffier

Tamara Corm and James Brett

Carolyn Dailey

Andrew Davenport

Karen and Ferdinand Groos

Harry Handelsman and
 Elizabeth Crompton-Batt

Maria de Madariaga and
 Anthony Vanger

Brian McMahon

Cate Olson and Nash Robbins

Kadee Robbins

Mike Servent

Cora and Kaveh Sheibani

Dasha Shenkman

Geoff Westmore and Paula
 Clemett

Helen and Edward White

THE COMPANY OF ANGELS

Contributors

ADONIS (né Ali Ahmad Said Esber) was born in Syria in 1930. As poet, critic, translator and essayist Adonis has published dozens of volumes, including the pioneering *An Introduction to Arab Poetics* and a multivolume anthology of Arabic poetry (*Diwan al-shi'r al-arabi*) that covers almost two millennia of verse and has been in print since its publication in 1964. Among Adonis's many awards are the Bjørnson Prize, the first International Nzim Hikmet Poetry Award, and the Syria–Lebanon Best Poet Award. In August 2011 Adonis became the first Arab writer to win Germany's prestigious Goethe Prize.

TEJU COLE, born in the US in 1975 and raised in Nigeria, is the author of two books: a novella, *Every Day is for the Thief*, and a novel, *Open City*, which won the PEN/Hemingway Award, was nominated for the National Book Critics Circle Award and the Royal Society of Literature's Ondaatje Prize, and was named one of the best books of 2011 by more than twenty magazines. He is Distinguished Writer in Residence at Bard College and is a contributor to the *New Yorker*, the *Atlantic*, *Brick* and *Granta*.

GEOFF DYER is the author of *Jeff in Venice, Death in Varanasi* and three previous novels, as well as many non-fiction books. Dyer has won the Somerset Maugham Prize, the Bollinger Everyman Wodehouse Prize for Comic Fiction, a National

Book Critics Circle Award, a Lannan Literary Award, the International Centre of Photography's 2006 Infinity Award for writing on photography, and the American Academy of Arts and Letters' E.M. Forster Award. His books have been translated into more than twenty languages. He lives in London.

MAYA JASANOFF is a professor of history at Harvard University. She is the author of *Edge of Empire: Conquest and Collecting in the East,* 1750–1850, which was awarded the 2005 Duff Cooper Prize, and *Liberty's Exiles: The Loss of America and the Remaking of the British Empire*, which won the 2012 National Book Critics Circle Award for Non-Fiction, the George Washington Book Prize and was shortlisted for the BBC Samuel Johnson Prize.

SVEN LINDQVIST is a major Swedish writer. Since 1955 he has published thirty books of essays, aphorisms, autobiography, documentary prose, travel and reportage. Many of these became the subject of Swedish literary and political controversy. Internationally, he is best known for his books on China, Latin America and Africa. He has a PhD in the History of Literature from Stockholm University, an honorary doctorate from Uppsala University and an honorary professorship from the Swedish government. He has two children, Aron and Clara. Since 1986 he has been married to Agneta Stark, a leading feminist economist.

ALAIN MABANCKOU was born in 1966 in the Congo. He currently lives in both LA and Paris, and teaches literature at UCLA. He is the author of six volumes of poetry and eight novels. He received the Subsaharan African Literature Prize for

Blue-White-Red and the Prix Renaudot for *Memoirs of a Porcu-pine*. He was selected by *Vanity Fair* as one of Africa's greatest living writers.

MICHAEL ONDAATJE is most recently the author of *The Cat's Table*. His other books include *The English Patient, Anil's Ghost, Coming through Slaughter, The Collected Works of Billy the Kid, Divisadero, Handwriting, The Cinnamon Peeler*, and *The Conversations: Walter Murch and the Art of Editing Film*. He is one of the editors of the literary magazine *Brick*. He was born in Sri Lanka and now lives in Canada.

CARYL PHILLIPS is an author and playwright. He has written numerous plays and documentaries for radio, film, theatre and television; nine novels, including *Dancing in the Dark*, which won the 2006 PEN/Beyond Margins Award, *A Distant Shore*, which won the 2004 Commonwealth Writers' Prize, and *Crossing the River*, which won the James Tait Black Memorial Prize and was shortlisted for the 1993 Booker Prize; and five works of non-fiction, including *A New World Order* and *Colour Me English*. His work has been translated into over a dozen languages.

KAMILA SHAMSIE was born in 1973 in Pakistan. She is the author of five previous novels: *In the City by the Sea, Kartography* (both shortlisted for the John Llewellyn Rhys Prize), *Salt and Saffron, Broken Verses* and *Burnt Shadows*, which was shortlisted for the Orange Prize and has been translated into more than twenty languages. Three of her novels have received awards from Pakistan's Academy of Letters. She lives in London and is a Fellow of the Royal Society of Literature and trustee of English PEN.

AHDAF SOUEIF, a citizen of Egypt and the UK, is the author of the bestselling *The Map of Love* (shortlisted for the Booker Prize in 1999 and translated into twenty-eight languages), as well the novel *In the Eye of the Sun* and a collection of short stories, *I Think of You*. A collection of her essays, *Mezzaterra: Fragments from the Common Ground*, was published in 2004, as was her translation (from Arabic into English) of Mourid Barghouti's *I Saw Ramallah*. She writes regularly for the *Guardian* in the UK and has a weekly column (in Arabic) in *al-Shorouk* in Egypt. In 2007 Soueif founded Engaged Events, a UK-based charity. Its first project was the Palestine Festival of Literature, which takes place in the occupied cities of Palestine and in Gaza. Her account of Egyptian events, *Cairo: My City, Our Revolution*, was published by Bloomsbury in January 2012. In 2010 she became the first recipient of the Mahmoud Darwich Award (Ramallah) and in 2012 was awarded the Constantin Cavafis Prize (Cairo/ Athens) as well as the Metropolis Bleu Award (Montreal).

COLM TÓIBÍN's novels include *The Master* and *Brooklyn*. He is a contributing editor at the *London Review of Books* and is the Irene and Sidney B. Silverman Professor of Humanities at Columbia University in New York.

JUAN GABRIEL VÁSQUEZ was born in Bogotá in 1973. He studied Latin American literature at the Sorbonne between 1996 and 1998, and now lives in Barcelona. *The Informers* (Bloomsbury, 2008), Vásquez's first novel to be translated into

English, was shortlisted for the Independent Foreign Fiction Prize. It was followed in 2011 by *The Secret History of Costaguana*, which won the Qwerty Prize in Barcelona, and *The Sound of Things Falling*, which won the Alfaguara prize in Madrid. In 2012 he was awarded the Prix Roger Caillois in Paris, previously awarded to writers such as Mario Vargas Llosa, Carlos Fuentes and Roberto Bolaño.

JEANETTE WINTERSON, OBE, is a writer. Her work has been published in twenty-two countries. Her latest book is the memoir: *Why Be Happy When You Could Be Normal?*

Copyright

All of the pieces in this volume were commissioned by Artangel and originally recorded as part of *A London Address* in the *Roi des Belges* on the roof of the Queen Elizabeth Hall.
www.artangel.org.uk/aroomforlondon

'Solo in the River Thames Orchestra' by Adonis. Copyright © Adonis 2013. Translation copyright © Khaled Mattawa 2013.

'Natives on the Boat' by Teju Cole. Copyright © Teju Cole 2013. This essay first appeared on the *New Yorker*'s Page-Turner blog, September 2012.

'Some Stories, with Annotations' by Geoff Dyer. Copyright © Geoff Dyer 2013. This essay first appeared as 'Ship Write' in *Guernica*, September 2012.

'A River Passage' by Maya Jasanoff. Copyright © Maya Jasanoff 2013.

'Bed and Breakfast' by Sven Lindqvist. Copyright © Sven Lindqvist 2013. An earlier version of this essay was published as the preface to *The Myth of Wu Tao-tzu* by Sven Lindqvist (Granta Books, 2012).

'London's Heart of Darkness' by Alain Mabanckou. Copyright © Alain Mabanckou 2013. Translation copyright © Sarah Ardizzone 2013.

'A Port Accent' by Michael Ondaatje. Copyright © Michael Ondaatje 2013. A portion of this essay was first published in *The Cat's Table* by Michael Ondaatje (Jonathan Cape, 2011).

'A Bend in the River' by Caryl Phillips. Copyright © Caryl Phillips 2013

Sources

INTRODUCTION | James Lingwood, Michael Morris

Conrad, Joseph, *Heart of Darkness* (Penguin, London, 2007).

REMEMBER THE FUTURE | Juan Gabriel Vásquez

Carroll, Lewis, *Alice in Wonderland* (Norton Critical Editions, New York, 1992).

Conrad, Joseph, *Heart of Darkness* (Everyman's Library, London, 1993).

Conrad, Joseph, *Lord Jim* (Everyman's Library, London, 1992).

Conrad, Joseph, *The Secret Agent* (Everyman's Library, London, 1992).

Karl, Frederick R. and Laurence Davies, eds, *The Collected Letters of Joseph Conrad* (Cambridge University Press, Cambridge, 1988).

A PLACE BEFORE THE FLOOD | Jeanette Winterson

Beckett, Samuel, *Happy Days*, from *The Complete Dramatic Works* (Faber, London, 2006).

Conrad, Joseph, *Heart of Darkness* (Penguin, London, 2007).

Duffy, Carol Ann, 'Snow', from *The Bees* (Picador, London, 2012).

BED AND BREAKFAST | Sven Lindqvist

London, Jack, *The People of the Abyss* (Echo Library, London, 2007).

A BEND IN THE RIVER | Caryl Phillips

Eliot, T. S., 'The Waste Land', from *The Waste Land and Other Poems* (Faber, London, 2002).

Selvon, Samuel, *The Lonely Londoners* (Penguin, London, 2006).

A RIVER PASSAGE | Maya Jasanoff

Conrad, Joseph, *Heart of Darkness* (Penguin, London, 2007).

Eliot, T. S., *The Four Quartets* (Faber, London, 2001).

Karl, Frederick R. and Laurence Davies, eds, *The Collected Letters of Joseph Conrad* (Cambridge University Press, Cambridge, 1988).

A PORT ACCENT | Michael Ondaatje

Caesar, Julius, *The Gallic War: Seven Commentaries on The Gallic War with an Eighth Commentary by Aulus Hirtius*, trans. Carolyn Hammond (Oxford University Press, Oxford, 2008).

Conrad, Joseph, *Heart of Darkness* (Penguin, London, 2007).

Gandhi, Mahatma, 'On My Way Home Again to India', from *The Vegetarian* (London, 16 April, 1892).

Ondaatje, Michael, *The Cat's Table* (Jonathan Cape, London, 2011).

Shanaathanan T., *The Incomplete Thombu* (Raking Leaves, Amsterdam, 2011).

SOME STORIES, WITH ANNOTATIONS | Geoff Dyer

Amis, Martin, *London Fields* (Jonathan Cape, London, 1989).

Benjamin, Walter, 'The Storyteller', from *Illuminations* (Pimlico, London, 1999).

Borges, Jorge Luis, 'Manuscript Found in a Book of Joseph Conrad', from *Selected Poems*, Vol. 2 (Penguin, London, 2000).

Céline, Louis-Ferdinand, *Journey to the End of the Night*, trans. Ralph Manheim (Alma Classics, London, 2012).

Conrad, Joseph, *Heart of Darkness* (Penguin, London, 2007).

Fitzgerald, F. Scott, *The Great Gatsby* (Penguin, London, 1992).

Fitzgerald, F. Scott, quoted by Matthew J. Bruccoli in *Some Sort of Epic Grandeur: The Life of F. Scott Fitzgerald* (Cardinal, London, 1991).

Fitzgerald, F. Scott, quoted by Matthew J. Bruccoli (ed.), *F. Scott Fitzgerald: A Life in Letters* (Simon and Schuster, New York, 1995).

Ginsberg, Allen, Liner Notes, from *Desire* by Bob Dylan (Columbia Records, 1976).

Lodge, David, *The British Museum is Falling Down* (Vintage, London, 2011).

Wells, H. G., quoted by V. S. Naipaul in 'Conrad's Darkness and Mine', in *Literary Occasions*, ed. Pankaj Mishra (Knopf, New York, 2003).

NATIVES ON THE BOAT | Teju Cole

Conrad, Joseph, *Heart of Darkness* (Penguin, London, 2007).

Naipaul, V. S., *The Enigma of Arrival* (Picador, London, 2002).

WAITING FOR THE FLOOD | Ahdaf Soueif

Conrad, Joseph, *Heart of Darkness* (Penguin, London, 2007).

A ROOM, WITH A VIEW, OF ONE'S OWN | Kamila Shamsie

Conrad, Joseph, *Heart of Darkness* (Penguin, London, 2007).

Woolf, Virginia, *The Common Reader*, Vol. 2 (Vintage, London, 2003).